AF477702

ALL GUTS AND NO GLORY

ALL GUTS AND NO GLORY

An Alabama Coach's Memoir of Desegregating College Athletics

BILL ELDER

NEWSOUTH BOOKS
Montgomery | Louisville

NewSouth Books
P.O. Box 1588
Montgomery, AL 36102

Library of Congress Cataloging-in-Publication Data

Elder, Bill, 1941-
All guts and no glory : an Alabama coach's memoir of desegregating
college athletics / Bill Elder.
p. cm.
Includes bibliographical references and index.
ISBN-13: 978-1-58838-209-2
ISBN-10: 1-58838-209-5
1. Elder, Bill, 1941- 2. Basketball coaches--Alabama--Biography.
3. Discrimination in sports--United States. 4. United States--Race
relations. I. Title.
GV884.E43A3 2007
796.323092--dc22
[B]
2007010950

Design by Randall Williams
Printed in the United States of America
by the Maple-Vail Book Manufacturing Group

To my wife and best friend, Vivian Logan Elder

To my daughters,
Laura Elder Gogis and Lacey Elder Montgomery

And to the young men who played for me at
Northeast State Junior College and who had the courage
to "stay the course" during those very dangerous days

CONTENTS

Photographs follow page 64

Acknowledgments

It is my sincere belief that all things happen for a reason. I had a story I felt needed to be told and worked for several years getting it down on paper. When I shared it with a few people in the literary community who were qualified and willing to offer an informed opinion, I was delighted that they agreed. But they also told me that I needed an editor who would work with me on such things as style, flow and structure so that the final product would be in publishable shape.

But where could I find one? As it turned out, several people suggested that I contact Jim Buford, who had published several creative works, and enlist him in my search. Jim read the manuscript and suggested that my editor needed to be someone who could identify with my experiences, shared my values, understood where I was coming from, and above all, would be faithful to my vision and purpose. He suggested several names and contacted a few people but never located anyone who we felt matched our requirements.

I suggested that based on our conversations, he should be the editor. He hesitated at first, but finally agreed to undertake the task. It was a good decision. Jim immersed himself in my manuscript and knew intuitively what I was trying to get across and worked diligently to get my work in order. He had the ability to sense what I intended to communicate and the skills to make it sound a lot better while using my words. It was a point of pride with Jim that it was my book, and unless he included a fact or anecdote to add color or to establish a historical context he always used my words. In the lexicon of my profession, I couldn't have found a better coach, and from a personal perspective, a better friend.

Prologue

*"If it weren't for the dark days, we wouldn't know
what it is to walk in the light"*
—EARL CAMPBELL
NFL All-Pro Running Back

Whether one attends games or watches them on television, it is obvious that the players in most sports are identified by the numbers on their uniforms rather than the color of their skin. At all levels—high school, college and professional—and especially in baseball, football and basketball—the sports with major national appeal—what matters is talent, not race. This is as it should be, but there was a time only a few decades ago when black players were rare in some sports and were not even allowed to play in others. Only in professional boxing were blacks allowed to compete on a more or less equal basis, and even then when a black fighter won the heavyweight title, there was always a "white hope" waiting to take it back and restore it to a rightful owner.

It was not until 1947 that Jackie Robinson signed with the Brooklyn Dodgers and broke baseball's "color line." By the late 1950s teams in professional sports were open to players of all races, as were college teams in most areas of the country, although the idea that blacks "had their place" would persist for many more years. For example, there were unwritten rules that blacks could not play quarterback in football, and the maximum number of black players on a basketball team was "three at home and four on the road."

In the South, however, the vestiges of a dual educational system remained for years after the U.S. Supreme Court ruled in 1954 that segregated schools were unconstitutional. In most places teams from "white" schools could not even play against teams from "black" schools at either the high school or college level. In 1959 the all-white Mississippi State basketball team had to defy the law to play in the NCAA tournament because the state legislature had passed a measure prohibiting competition between white and black players. Southern resistance to integration also kept major league professional sports out of the region until 1965 when the Milwaukee Braves moved to Atlanta and the city acquired an expansion team in the NFL.

Black participation in sports at predominantly white educational institutions at any level could be described as tokenism at best until the late 1960s, and before that time black athletes were not recruited by either the Southeastern or Atlantic Coast conferences. Talented players either went to the Big 10 or PAC 10 or played for historically black colleges, including Sam "Bam" Cunningham, a running back from Mobile who earned All-American honors at Southern California. As fate would have it, Alabama, coached by the legendary Paul "Bear" Bryant, lost to Southern California in 1970 in a game in which Cunningham ran for 135 yards and two touchdowns. The following year Bryant began to actively recruit black players. He and his basketball counterpart, C. M. Newton, are credited with bringing the University of Alabama (and the SEC) into the modern era, although Don Haskins, basketball coach at

Texas Western, had issued a wake-up call in 1966 to the great Adolph Rupp.

That was the year the Miners, with a squad of black players, won the national championship by defeating a heavily favored and all-white team from Kentucky in the finals of the NCAA tournament. The game, which is celebrated in the movie *Glory Road*, is said to have changed college basketball in America, although teams with mostly black players had won championships in previous years. Whether or not the game was a watershed in basketball history, it got the attention of Southern coaches, although when Rupp retired in 1972, Kentucky still did not have one black player.

Almost everything I have related is known to many people who follow sports and is certainly familiar to all sports historians. This is because the people and events portrayed were major stories in the national media. There is another common thread that runs through these stories. With the possible exception of Branch Rickey, the general manager of the Brooklyn Dodgers who signed Jackie Robinson, the people who made the decisions that brought black players into the mainstream of athletics did not have altruistic motives. The thing uppermost in the minds of Joe Gibbs, Bear Bryant, C. M. Newton, and Don Haskins was winning, not bringing about social change. And without detracting from their accomplishments, it should be pointed out that none of these coaches faced the kind of white backlash that generally accompanied the integration of Southern sports.

For sure, Bear Bryant got some hate mail and Don Haskins and his players had their lives threatened. But they had already reached, or were near, the pinnacle of success at Division I colleges. Their loyal followers vastly outnumbered their detractors.

Even after Coach Bryant began to integrate the football team at Alabama, he remained the most popular figure in the state. The good ole boys who used the N-word still thought he hung the moon. Even though most of them had never even been to Tuscaloosa, they still proudly displayed an Alabama decal on the rear window of their pickups next to the Confederate Battle Flag.

There were other coaches and their players in junior colleges and small institutions in Alabama and the South whose stories played out mostly under the radar of the national media. Their contact with the true believers in segregation was up-close and personal, a fact especially true for those who coached basketball. The games were not played in ten thousand-seat coliseums where the crowds included a good contingent of college students whose racial views were considerably more advanced than those in the general population. Rather, they were played in small arenas in front of a few hundred people, many of whom did not take kindly to social change. If they wanted to offer the coach some friendly advice as to why integration was unacceptable in "their" community, they had his home phone number. If the coach continued down the wrong path and it became necessary to carry out certain late-night activities to show him the error of his ways, they also had his street address.

I was one of those coaches. I entered this profession in 1965 because being a student-athlete had taught me the benefits of hard work, discipline, and teamwork and given me an appreciation for values such as respect, responsibility, leadership, and integrity and for the importance of the relationship between mind and body in reaching one's full potential. I believed that I had the knowledge and skills to build a winning team while providing athletes a positive, character-building experience. I did not set out on a mission to battle racism and reform society, but as a Christian I did realize it was my duty to give equal opportunity to young athletes with ability, regardless of race, in my recruiting, coaching, and teaching roles.

My experiences were not that different from those of others in my profession, and I believe that all of us, along with our players, contributed as much to removing the barriers to equality in college athletics as did our counterparts with a higher profile. I hope that by recounting the people, places and events of my journey through those turbulent times, I will increase the realization that in sports, as well as any other field of endeavor, tolerating injustice to anyone diminishes everyone, and for better or worse, we are all in this together.

A White Boy in the Land of Opportunity

"All opportunities are equal, but some opportunities are more equal than others."
—Anonymous

It was 1944 and I was about three years old when a sense of place began to form in my mind. The place was Birmingham, and as time went by, I came to understand that it was located in America, the best country in the world. It was the country that was fighting a war so people everywhere could be free, like people in America had always been. By late 1945, the war was over and America was the land of opportunity where the future was bright and the opportunities were unlimited. Soldiers, sailors, and Marines who had fought in the war were coming home to find good-paying jobs. Soon they would buy new cars, get married, build houses in the suburbs, and begin to raise families. For those who had stayed behind and taken care of the home front, the days of gas rationing, victory gardens, and air raid drills gave way to postwar prosperity. The economic boom meant that a person could go anywhere, start a business, and possibly make a fortune. My dad thought so, and our family moved to Marion, Ohio, where he had obtained a franchise to bottle Dr Pepper and Orange Crush. America was the "great melting pot," and it seemed that people of all races could share in the American Dream because we were all created equal. But as is often the case, things were not what they seemed.

The first black person I ever knew was Mima, a lady who took care of my brother Owen and me when we still lived in Birmingham and also did some light housework for my parents. I remember her as a friendly person who cared very much for us and whom we loved very much. I was told that Mima actually had a degree from a college in the Midwest and was a teacher at one of the local black elementary schools, but the pay was so low that she and many others had to take part-time jobs to survive. The fact that a black teacher had to perform domestic work to make ends meet seems beyond comprehension today, but at the time it was accepted as the natural order of things in the South. It was actually a separate and unequal version of the American Dream where the word "separate" meant what it said, and some people were apparently more equal than others.

The metaphor of the melting pot comes from the idea that America is a nation of immigrants and is expressed in the lines of a poem that used to be recited by elementary school children: "It doesn't matter what your skin, you simply melt right in." After we moved to Ohio, my brother and I soon discovered that it wasn't quite that simple. My father had rented an old building in a poor section of town close to the railroad tracks and purchased some used bottling equipment to get the business up and running. Since the business was truly a mom and pop operation, both of my parents worked long hours at the plant. They were putting all of the money that they could back into the business. Hiring a babysitter to take care of my brother and me when they were at work was out of the question. With this in mind, my brother and I spent a significant amount of our time playing in and around the plant. One day we decided to go exploring in the neighborhood that surrounded the bottling business. There was a small church about a hundred yards down the street. Being an adventurous pair, we went in the church basement through a back door that we found unlocked.

After looking around for a few minutes, we heard footsteps on the stairs leading down to the basement and suddenly we were confronted by five black boys. They appeared to be a few years older than my brother, who was eight years old at the time. They looked at us and we looked at them for what seemed to be two or three minutes, but in reality, was probably only a few seconds. The biggest boy was the first one to say anything. "We want to know what you two white boys are doing in our church basement," he demanded. We could tell from the tone of his voice that we were not welcome. "Our parents run the bottling plant down the street and we are just looking around the neighborhood," my brother answered, hoping to defuse the situation. But we could tell from the black boy's expression that the excuse was not good enough. "We're going to beat you up," he stated. My brother still thought maybe he could talk his way out of our dilemma. "We're not hurting anything," he said plaintively.

Apparently the boy decided that we at least deserved to know what we had done wrong. "We're going to beat you up because you are white boys and you are not allowed in this neighborhood. It is for black people only," he explained in a loud voice. After hearing that, my brother pulled out his wallet and offered it to the boy, saying he could keep it if he would let us go. The older boy took the wallet, which we took as a "yes" and then bolted for the door and made our escape. Of course there is a possibility that he would have given the wallet back to my brother and then, along with his friends, beaten us up anyway, but some things it is better not to know. What I did learn from that experience was that skin color did matter in the melting pot, and that mistreating others because of their race was not something done only by white people. Prejudice is where you find it, even in Ohio in the basement of a black church.

Although my first experience was on the receiving end of prejudicial behavior, this was rarely the case. During my growing-up years I observed overt discrimination in the South and a somewhat more subtle form in the Midwest. Since most of our relatives still lived in the South, we frequently made trips back to Birmingham. On one of these visits when I was seven years old, I went shopping with my mother and our relatives. We were in Loveman's, a large department store in downtown Birmingham, when I noticed that there were two water fountains located on a wall next to the bathrooms. I thought that that was odd; why would a store have two water fountains located side by side? I went over to one of the fountains and started to drink when my mother came rushing over, clearly flustered. "Bill, you have to drink out of the other fountain," she said, with a tone of urgency. I thought there must be something wrong with the fountain but it was not that at all. "That one is for colored people," she said in a low voice. "The other one is for white people. If you will look above each fountain, you will see there are signs that say 'whites only' or 'colored only.'" Shortly after drinking my fill of water, I had to go to the bathroom. When I asked my mother where the bathrooms were, she pointed to the wall next to the children's clothes. "Look at the signs and be sure that you go into the 'whites only' bathroom," she admonished me. But it didn't end with segregated drinking fountains and bathrooms. It was also in Loveman's that I had my first opportunity to eat at a soda fountain and it was a great treat. You could spin on the stools while you watched the waiters cook your food and prepare your soft drink. I was having a great time when I noticed a sign on the wall behind the soda fountain area that said, "Service for whites only."

While eating my lunch, I asked my mother why blacks and whites drink out of separate water fountains, use separate bathrooms, and eat in different places. My mother hesitated for several seconds, choosing her words carefully. "Some colored people are not clean and they leave germs on water fountains, toilet seats, and eating utensils," she explained, but I could sense that somehow she knew this was not right.

As I grew older my lifelong interest in sports began to take hold. We continued to visit Birmingham and I became a fan of the Birmingham Barons. This was when there were only sixteen major league teams, and the talent pool dipped down into the Class AA Southern Association. Birmingham was the last stop on the road to the major leagues for future stars such as Jimmy Piersall and Walt Dropo. During the late 1940s the annual home attendance for Barons' games approached a half million, more than a number of major league teams could claim. During a hot pennant race, it was not unusual for fifteen thousand or more fans to pack Rickwood Field for a game with the Atlanta Crackers, the Barons' major rival.

When I was nine years old, my dad and I took a bus from my grandfather's house to a Barons' game. I immediately noticed that the seating on the bus was divided between white and black people by signs placed on the backs of the seats.

Black people sat behind the signs in the seats toward the back of the bus and the white people sat in the front. After we arrived at Rickwood Field and took our seats for the game with the Atlanta Crackers, I noticed that there was a small section behind the right field fence where all the black people sat. It also had a separate ticket window and entrance gate.

After watching a few innings, I asked my dad why the black people were all sitting in the right field section of the bleachers. He thought about it for a while and then said, "The blacks sit there during the Barons' games but they can sit where they want to for the Black Barons' games." He explained further: "The Black Barons play at Rickwood when the Barons are playing on the road and travel when the Barons are at home."

He never really explained why the blacks could not sit where they wanted to when the Barons were playing. He went on to say that the Black Barons had a great young player by the name of Willie Mays and that white people went to the Black Barons' games sometimes to watch him play. I asked if the white people had to sit in the right field section for the Black Barons' games, and he indicated that the blacks and whites sat together at those games. Even at that young age, I recognized the inconsistency that black people were required to sit in the right field sections for the Barons' games while whites were permitted to sit where they wanted when the Black Barons were playing.

Although I didn't know it at the time, the Black Barons formed the cornerstone of professional Negro baseball in the South. Arising from Birmingham's active industrial leagues, in 1920 the club became a charter franchise in the Negro Southern League. Through its long history the club was at various times associated with the Negro Southern League, the Negro National League, and finally the Negro American League, the pinnacle of Negro professional baseball. The team's heyday came in the 1940s when the Black Barons fielded exceptionally strong teams featuring such stars as Piper Davis, Lester Lockett, Artie Wilson, and Ed Steele, winning several pennants. It seems somewhat ironic that the city of Birmingham, which has worked so long to get a major league sports franchise, had one with the Black Barons thirty years before the Braves moved to Atlanta.

On the bus on the way back to my granddad's house after the game, I asked my dad why the black people were required to sit in the back of the bus. "One of the reasons is that there might be trouble if the blacks sat with the whites," he answered. I asked him what he meant by "trouble," but he never really explained other than to say that there had been some incidents where some black people had cut white people with razors on the buses. After riding for a while in silence, we drove past what looked like an elementary school complete with swings, slides, and a playground. I asked my dad if that was the school that I would attend if we lived in my grandfather's house. "No, that is where the black children go to school," he explained. "The white school is located several blocks away." I wanted to ask him why the black and white children went to different schools, but I could tell that he didn't want to spend any more time on that subject. And besides, I had pretty much figured out the answer.

The following Sunday, my brother and I, along with my mother and grandmother, went to the Baptist church where my grandmother was a member. The topic of the Sunday school class that we attended was how Jesus loves everyone. The teacher used a flannel board as a visual aid for the class.

He first attached a likeness of Jesus on the board. He then added figures of white, black, Indian, Asian, and Hispanic children around Jesus. He went on to explain that Jesus loves all of the children in the world, regardless of race. We finished the class by singing a popular song recorded by the Cowboy Church Sunday School, a group that was popular on WVOK radio. I can still remember the words: "Red and yellow, black and white, they are equal in His sight. Jesus loves the little children of the world."

After Sunday school class my brother and I walked up the steps from the basement room to the sanctuary of the church. We joined my grandmother and mother at my grandmother's usual seat in the third pew from the pulpit on the right. After singing a few songs and taking the offering, the pastor spoke on the church's missionary efforts in Africa. He talked about how we should support the missionary family that the church was sponsoring. He talked in detail about how the family was ministering to the people of a village in Africa. He mentioned that many of these people had never heard the word of God and how important it was for the church to remember the missionaries in prayer as well as to support them financially. He concluded by showing some slides of the missionaries working with the people in their village. I could see on the slides that the missionaries were the only white people there. The rest of the people were black.

On the way home, I asked my grandmother if black people were allowed to come to their church if they sat in a separate area such as the balcony. My mother quickly interrupted the conversation. "Bill, sometimes you ask too many questions. The black people have their own churches that they go to. You need to be quiet and let the adults talk," she added emphatically.

That night I had trouble going to sleep on the roll-out sofa that I shared with my brother in the living room of my grandparents' house. Usually I was kept awake by the trains that rumbled through at all hours on the tracks that were located no more that thirty yards from the house. Tonight, however, was different. I was confused by what I was continuing to see in Birmingham. I had learned that black people in Birmingham were not permitted to sit in the same areas with white people on the bus or at baseball games; that black people had separate bathrooms and could not eat at the same restaurants with whites; that black children went to different school than white kids; that churches were sending missionaries to spread the word of God to black people in Africa, but blacks here were not allowed to go the same churches as white people.

I knew most of my relatives in Birmingham were hard-working, kindhearted, and law-abiding people. I could not understand how they could justify treating black people like this and then send missionaries to Africa to try to teach them the word of God. I wondered how one could believe that Jesus loves all of us equally and still believe in segregation or think that one race is better than another. Later I would learn that many Southern ministers believed that whites were created by God as a superior race and that contacts with blacks were authorized by Him only for the purpose of converting them from their heathen ways. Whites were required to avoid mingling socially with blacks so they would remain "pure." In other words the "Jim Crow" segregation laws were not passed merely to enforce local customs and to keep black people in their place. They were necessary to carry out God's divine will. This just did not add up in my young mind.

On our way back to Ohio from Birmingham, we stopped

for lunch at a barbeque restaurant in Decatur, Alabama. We always made at least one stop at the popular eating establishment on these trips, and I always looked forward to it. After we gave the waitress our orders, I began looking around and noticed a sign near the cash register that said: "We reserve the right to make the choice of whom we serve." After we finished eating my brother and I went out in the parking lot to wait for our parents to pay the bill. While waiting, I noticed several black men ordering food out of a carryout window located on the side of the building. I already knew that black people were not allowed to eat in the same restaurants with whites. I now had learned that white people in the South would sell black people food as long as they didn't stay around to eat it. I had more questions for my parents but decided to keep them to myself for the rest of our vacation, not bringing up anything else about the "black and white situation."

Our bottling business in Marion was not doing well financially, and soon after we returned from our trip to Birmingham, my dad obtained a Sun Crest franchise in Bucyrus, a town about eighteen miles north. There was a severe housing shortage in Bucyrus so we ended up moving into a small apartment above the plant. Most of our neighbors worked for wages and, like my family, were what sociologists would call "lower middle class." But the economy was getting better and local manufacturing plants were gearing up for peacetime production and would soon begin to offer higher-paying jobs. There was a spirit of optimism that good times were just around the corner. This was the way it went for my dad who gave up the bottling business and, in spite of having only an eighth-grade education, passed the exam for a stationary engineer's license and went on to enjoy a successful career with the Timkin Roller Bearing Corporation.

All things considered, Bucyrus was a good place to grow up. I was blessed with athletic ability and never had to endure the childhood agony of being the "last one chosen" in pick-up games. From there I made the transition to Little League and other organized sports and was chosen for various all-star teams. Because I was more interested in making jump shots and throwing strikes than in studying long division, my performance in school was only average. My teachers, however, had another explanation for my lackluster performance: it was because I was from the South.

Poor white families from Kentucky and Tennessee often came to places like Bucyrus in search of better jobs. Looking back, most of these families were probably from the Appalachian areas of those states, which were populated by some of the poorest people in the United States. I know that I was treated differently by teachers in elementary school because of being a Southerner. In early grades, I was always put in the "slow" reading groups, usually before the teacher even heard me read. Most of the teachers just assumed that children from the South were not very smart. The teachers would give names to these groups such as the Blue Birds, Robins, Red Birds, etc. All of the children, however, immediately recognized that one group was for the slow learners, another for the intermediate learners, and a third for the brightest kids.

One of my most memorable examples of a teacher's prejudiced attitude toward Southerners is an event that happened in my ninth-grade biology class. I was sitting in class daydreaming about the upcoming freshman team basketball game with arch rival Galion when our teacher, Miss Grace Hibarger, started lecturing on why people from the South talked more slowly than those from the North. Being a Southerner, I perked up and actually started paying attention. She began by saying that some people thought Southerners talked and moved slowly because of the oppressive heat that lasted much of the year in that region of the country. According to her, this was a good theory but it simply was not true. She said the real reason was that most people in the South did not have indoor bathrooms and when they felt the need to go to the bathroom, they simply went outside to urinate or defecate on the ground. Since they also did not wear shoes, they eventually stepped in their own feces and contracted worms. They became infected by the worms, which in turn caused them to talk and move more slowly; this was also the cause of their lower intellect, she said.

I was the only person from the South in that class, and all of my classmates knew this. After Miss Hibarger finished her lecture on this subject, many of the boys and girls in the class began looking at me like I was an alien. It was a humiliating experience, to say the least. I knew I had never seen a house in the South that did not have indoor plumbing. I had never seen anyone go out into the yard to use the bathroom. I also knew that my cousin had graduated from Tulane University Medical School and that he certainly was smarter that Miss Hibarger.

The problem was that many of my classmates seemed to believe this nonsense and I felt that they looked down on me. I was automatically considered an inferior student and felt that I had to prove otherwise to be accepted. It was basically the same mindset that even today stereotypes people because of their race. During those times it was common to refer to a black person who had succeeded at something as "a credit to his race." Maybe my teacher thought I should strive to be "a credit to my region." This experience and others reinforced the strong feelings that I already had against prejudice in any form. I also learned firsthand a little bit of what black people have had to deal with on a much larger scale.

Unlike Birmingham, public accommodations in Bucyrus were not segregated. Black people could eat, attend ball games, ride buses, go to movies, attend school, and carry on their daily activities without being treated like second-class citizens. The relatively small number of black residents had good incomes and lived in middle- to upper middle-class neighborhoods. In retrospect, however, I realize that discrimination was still a fact of life for many black people in Ohio, especially in the larger cities, which in some ways were as segregated as Birmingham. Neighborhoods were generally all one race, the black neighborhoods being the ones with badly maintained streets, poor-quality services, and inferior schools. People from these neighborhoods could not compete effectively for good-paying jobs and typically took manual and semi-skilled work. The term used later to describe this was de facto segregation, and it would persist long after the "Jim Crow" laws of the South were a distant memory.

Occasionally something happened that reminded me of the overt discrimination that I had observed in the South. Once, when I was ten years old, I went with my parents to an American Legion baseball game. It was in the early 1950s and baseball was the national game. It was always a great treat for me to see the older boys play the game that I loved. The routine for my friends and me at the games was to chase foul balls that went out of the playing area. A wheat field ran along the third-base side of the field behind the grandstands. The wheat was usually several feet high during baseball season, and since the grass in the playground area was not frequently cut, it was usually at least six to eight inches high. A fouled-off pitch often resulted in the proverbial "lost ball in the high weeds," and if not recovered, it cost Red Widman, the coach, $1.25 to replace it. This was a considerable sum in those days, so he paid us kids a nickel for each foul ball that we found and returned. Since that was the price of a Coke, it seemed like a good deal for both the coach and the kids.

Usually there were four or five of my friends from the neighborhood at the games. One of my friends was Jimmy Slaughter, a young black boy who played with me in my youth baseball league. He was very well mannered and fun to be around. Even at ten years of age, I was aware that his family had more money than we did. They lived in a nice home in a middle-class neighborhood. Jimmy was always well dressed and had top-notch sporting equipment.

During lulls in the "foul ball" action, my buddies and I frequently engaged in friendly wrestling matches. Jimmy and I started wrestling one night not too far from the bleachers where my parents were sitting. As usual, we ended up laughing, lying in the grass in an exhausted heap. I looked up in the stands and saw my mother motioning vigorously for me to come to her, so I climbed up to where she was sitting. "Bill, I do not want you wrestling with that black boy," she said sternly. When I asked why and pointed out that he was one of my friends from the youth baseball league, she hesitated and then said, "It is just not right for little white boys to be wrestling with little black boys."

I was taken aback by what my mother said. I had not even thought of Jimmy as being different than I was. He was just one of the guys I played with. Looking back at this incident, I realize that Jimmy was a much better person than any of the white kids that I was playing with that night. Even though I did not agree with what my mother said, I obeyed her and did not wrestle with Jimmy the rest of the night. I am sure he wondered why I avoided him and what he had done to upset me. We avoided talking about what had happened, but from then on our relationship was different.

Later that summer some family friends from Birmingham came to visit us in Bucyrus. They had a son my brother's age, and the day after they arrived, we went to Aumiller Park, a popular place for families to picnic, swim, play tennis, watch softball games, play horseshoes, play on the playground equipment, or just hang out. On a moment's notice my mother would often pack up the meal that we were getting ready to eat and we would head out to the park.

After finishing the picnic lunch that day, we all headed for the swimming pool. It was especially fun when my mother and dad decided to put on their out-of-date bathing suits and make the plunge into the always frigid water of the Aumiller Park Municipal Pool. Both families emerged from the dressing rooms about the same time and we all jumped into the pool together. We had been in the water about fifteen minutes when a black family came out of the dressing rooms and got in the water. The father of that family owned several small businesses and they lived in a very nice section of town. Their children were a little older than I so I did not know them very well, but I did know they were very popular at school. The only thing different about them is that they were black.

I had been in the pool with them before and did not think anything about it. Immediately after seeing them enter the pool, however, the family who was visiting with us got out of the pool, dressed, and went to our car. Since they were our guests, we had to get dressed and give them a ride back to our house. Even though my parents did not say anything about the reason our friends got out of the pool, it was obvious what had caused them to leave. I overheard their father say to my parents later that night, "I do not know about you, but we don't swim with niggers in Alabama."

When I was in the seventh grade at Bucyrus Junior High School, Herb Jones was the hometown sports hero. He was an outstanding football, basketball, and baseball player for the Bucyrus High School Redmen. All of my friends were in awe of his accomplishments. He was an excellent student and very popular with his classmates; in fact, during his senior year, he was elected president of the student government association for the entire school. After graduation, he went on to play college athletics. He was a true "student-athlete."

Herb was a young black man whose family had lived in Bucyrus for many years. His dad owned several hauling and garbage-collection businesses. They lived in what was considered one of the middle-class neighborhoods in town. Their home, like many in that neighborhood, was a roomy two-story white wooden structure. Their yard, shrubs, and flower garden were always immaculate.

During his senior year in high school, Herb started dating a very attractive white girl. She was a striking blonde and a member of the cheerleading squad and the homecoming court. Like Herb, she was one of the most popular students in her class. Their relationship was the source of much controversy. Public opinion concerning this relationship was, for the most part, evenly divided. One side took the position that interracial dating was wrong and that someone should put a stop to it. The other side thought that there was nothing wrong with their dating and everyone should just mind their own business. Regardless of which side you were on, the situation was the source of much heated conversation.

Like almost everyone else in town, I had heard about what had been called the "interracial dating situation," but I was not particularly concerned. Herb was one of my heroes and all I was interested in was what he was doing to help the Redmen win. My thoughts on the situation were that he had grown up with all his classmates. They had all gone to the same elementary, junior high, and high school. Most had known each other since they were six years old. Herb and the young lady were both good people from good families. Herb seemed to me to be a better person than many of the older boys that I knew, so what was the problem? Eventually, it became clear to me that racial prejudice knows no geographical boundaries. In Alabama it was pretty much out in the open. In Ohio, it was often just below the surface, but ready to break through any time.

During those days it had become clear that I had considerable natural ability in athletics, and soon the days of Little League and recreation team sports would be behind me. When I was in the ninth grade, I started thinking about a career in athletics. Danny Bumstead, a young man who lived across the street from me, played professional baseball during the spring and summer and varsity basketball at Kenyon College during the fall and winter. Inspired by Danny's accomplishments, I secretly set a goal to play both professional baseball and college basketball. I also decided that after my baseball career was over, I would become a basketball coach.

I knew that black people were less likely to encounter

discrimination in sports, probably because that was the one place where talent mattered more than skin color, but there was still the occasional incident. And I continued to observe discrimination in its most blatant forms on our family trips back to Alabama. But things were about to change.

In December of 1955, a black woman named Rosa Parks was arrested on a city bus in Montgomery, Alabama, for refusing a driver's order to move to the back of the bus. The incident would set off the famous Montgomery Bus Boycott and bring the Rev. Martin Luther King, Jr., into the national spotlight. The modern civil rights movement had begun and there would be no turning back. Within a few years all the "white only" signs in the South would come down, and ultimately the economic barriers to equal opportunity in the rest of the country would begin to give way. It would be overstating things to say, however, that the elementary school poem that begins with "No matter what your skin" is completely accurate, even today. Skin color still matters, but thankfully, not as much.

Hardwood Warrior

*"Even when I'm old and gray and won't be able
to play it, I'll still love the game."*
—MICHAEL JORDAN
NBA Superstar

In the mid 1950s, Ike was president, Cokes cost a nickel, and baseball was the national pastime. Red-blooded American boys wanted to grow up and play in the major leagues. We each had dreams of being the next Joe DiMaggio and winning the World Series with a ninth inning home run, or possibly becoming a twenty-game winner like Whitey Ford. In Ohio we had the Cleveland Indians, and we followed sluggers Al Rosen and Larry Doby, along with strikeout king Bob Feller. If baseball was not our game, we would play football at Ohio State under the legendary coach Woody Hayes where All-American running back Howard "Hopalong" Cassidy led the Buckeye offense that was famous for its "three yards and a cloud of dust."

However, in Ohio we also had a legend of college basketball, long before the sport achieved national prominence. He was Clarence "Bevo" Francis, who played at tiny Rio Grande, a junior college with three classroom buildings, a gym without a shower room, and a total student body of ninety-four. Francis led the Rio Grande Redmen to thirty-nine straight victories and nearly rewrote the record books in the process. He averaged almost fifty points per game and once scored one hundred and sixteen points in a single game. During his second season Rio Grande defeated such national powerhouses as Creighton, Wake Forest, and Providence. Francis is credited for restoring the image of the game, which was under a dark cloud because of gambling scandals; in fact, many sports historians consider him the first true superstar of college basketball.

Francis, after junior college, decided not to transfer to a four-year college, instead signing a contract with the Boston Whirlwinds, the all-white team that toured with (and always lost to) the Harlem Globetrotters. Later Francis played several years in the Eastern League but never made it to the NBA and soon faded into obscurity. But his star continued to burn bright in Ohio, and basketball, which had been something to do to keep active between football and baseball, had become a real sport. In Bucyrus we had a special connection with Bevo. Rio Grande was only 150 miles away, and our high school nickname was also the Redmen. Kids involved in pick-up games, youth leagues, and even high school varsities all wanted to be like Bevo. I had the same aspirations along with a reasonable amount of athletic ability. What I didn't have, however, was height. By the end of my eighth-grade year, I was barely five feet tall.

As a pitcher and third baseman, I helped our team win the first-ever Bucyrus Little League City Championship. I was one of the league's top hitters and also pitched a one-hitter against one of our arch rivals, the Kiwanis squad. In football I made the junior high team in the seventh and eighth grades, but I was never a starter. In basketball I made the team, but it was late in the season of my eighth grade year before I saw any playing time. Although I still dreamed of following in Bevo's footsteps and being a basketball star, I mainly warmed the bench and wondered how long it would be before I finally got my growth spurt.

It didn't take much longer. By the time I entered the ninth grade, I had grown five inches. I became a starting guard for the ninth-grade football team. In basketball I came into my own and was the second leading scorer on the freshman team. As a sophomore I was starting guard on the junior varsity football team and second leading scorer on the JV basketball team. During my junior year I became a starter on the varsity in both football and basketball, where I averaged fourteen points per game once I joined the first team late in the season. Although the school dropped baseball, the county had an American Legion baseball program, and I was able to continue playing. As the starting second baseman, I hit over .300 on teams that won two straight county championships.

During my senior year I played guard on the football team, which was considered one of the better teams in the state, although there were no play-offs during that time. I continued to play American Legion baseball the summer after my senior year and ended the season with a batting average over .350. In basketball I averaged 18.3 points a game and was chosen for all-conference and all-area teams. The highlight of that year came when I broke Danny Bumstead's single-game scoring record.

In Ohio, all levels of organized sports were open to all races, and skin color mattered little in athletic competition. The community was happy to have black athletes represent Bucyrus High School, even though, as I mentioned earlier, people were less open-minded about their dating white girls. From recreation leagues to high school varsity, I played alongside and/or against black athletes in every sport.

Probably my most memorable experience along these lines was in basketball during my senior year; it came when we played against all-black Dayton Roosevelt High School, one of the top teams in the state. We met the "Teddies," as they were called, in a regular-season home game and were badly beaten. In addition to blowing us out on our own court, they brought a large contingent of fans along who cheered "We are the Teddies, the mighty, mighty Teddies" every time their team scored. During my college playing days and later when I was coaching, that cheer would ring in my ears whenever my team was having a bad night.

In the spring of my senior year, I received a modest number of scholarship offers to play football or basketball in college, and later I was scouted by the Philadelphia Phillies and Cleveland Indians. The Indians actually invited me to come to Municipal Stadium and work out before the start of the Indians' game. The only uniform they could find to fit me had belonged to Jimmy Piersall, whom I had watched when he played for the Birmingham Barons before being called up to the major leagues. Getting to take batting and infield practice in a major-league uniform was, however, as far as I ever got in professional baseball.

My choices were limited to football and basketball, and of the two, basketball was my favorite sport and the one in which I believed I had the most potential. My mother told me she thought it would be best if I want to a Christian school for at least one year. After that she would consider letting me transfer to a secular school to play sports. Wheaton College, located near Chicago, and Cedarville College in Ohio both met my mother's requirements, and both actively recruited me. Wheaton was and remains today the Harvard of Christian colleges, and moreover, had recently won the small-college national basketball championship. Cedarville, on the other hand, was just beginning to establish itself in academic and athletic circles. There was no doubt that Wheaton was where I wanted to go.

The Wheaton coach drove down from Chicago and offered me a place on the team subject to my scoring high enough on the College Boards (predecessor to the SAT and ACT) to be admitted. The test was scheduled on the Saturday morning after my last high school basketball game. I stayed out late that night and had to get up early to make the twenty-five-mile drive to Heidelberg College in Tiffin, Ohio, where the test was administered. I had two problems with the test. First, I was immature and didn't understand how important it was for me to do well. Secondly, I was sleep deprived and somewhat run-down from a long basketball season. In about two weeks I got a call from the coach. He said I hadn't scored high enough to be admitted and my only alternative was to enroll in summer school and make acceptable grades.

After thinking about this for a while, my parents and I decided it was best to accept the scholarship offer to play for the Cedarville Yellow Jackets. I played under two coaches at Cedarville, Sherwin Bowser and Don Callan. Both were proponents of a fast-break style of offense without much defense. We mainly played "run and gun" with the goal of just outscoring our opponents. I started off playing on the junior varsity team and then progressed to also dressing out with the varsity during my first year. I was actually playing the whole junior varsity game and seeing some additional action on the varsity on most nights. One night early in the season, I played the entire junior varsity game and then the coach put me in the varsity game five minutes into the contest and I played the rest of that game. It never dawned on me that I should be tired. I got to play two games in one night. "What could be better?" I remember thinking to myself. After that night, I got promoted to the varsity and became an on-and-off starter before the season ended.

Cedarville College (now Cedarville University) competed at a level comparable to today's National Association of Intercollegiate Athletics, or NAIA. While we did not play against major colleges, we did play Rio Grande, which was very meaningful to me because I had been such a fan of Bevo Francis. By then his playing days were over and he had returned home, but he still attended games. I was in hopes that I would do something to attract his attention, but unfortunately, that never happened. Maybe the only reason he didn't ever congratulate me was that he was busy signing autographs and couldn't get away. Then again, maybe not.

Cedarville traditionally faced some of the best historically black institutions in the nation—teams such as Kentucky State, Tennessee State, Central State, and Wilberforce University, its parent institution. At that time opportunities for black schools to play at major colleges were limited in the Midwest and non-existent in the South, although their athletes were capable of playing at any level. However, my most humbling experience playing against black athletes was not in either basketball or baseball; rather it was in tennis. I had never played organized tennis growing up, but I picked up the game quickly and made the college team. Before long I was the number two singles player. I was feeling pretty good about myself when we went to Central State for a match, but my opponent brought me down to earth, beating me 6-1, 6-1. That was bad enough, but he did it without ever taking off his warm-up suit.

One of our best basketball players was Dozier Carter, a gifted black athlete, who, at six feet, five inches and 225 pounds, had been a heavily recruited blue-chip prospect in both football and basketball. It was my understanding that Dozier passed up many offers to come to Cedarville because his parents wanted him to attend a Christian college. I learned the hard way that Dozier was both quick and strong. Once in practice when I had driven around my man and was wide open for a layup under the basket, Dozier left his man and rejected my shot before the ball left my hand. Although it was a clean block, he did it with such force that it broke the metatarsal in my right hand and I was out for four weeks. It was unintentional, and he was as upset about the incident as I was, and I assured him that I understood he meant no harm. "Things like that happen," I said through the pain, although what I was thinking was, "Next time let it happen to somebody else."

Official policies at Cedarville were based on the Scriptures. Students were held to high standards of moral conduct and were expected not to lie, cheat, or steal. We were required to attend a chapel service five days per week and both morning and evening services on Sunday. We were instructed in sermons that as Christians, we should not have sex before marriage, and we were advised not to date people who were not saved. The college subscribed to the principle that people of all races were created equal and discrimination was not to be tolerated. But there were certain exceptions. Students were not allowed to date members of another race, saved or not.

During my freshman year, the administration learned that a black male was dating a fellow student who was white. The word around campus was that the two were given an ultimatum: either end their relationship or be expelled. The students complied with the demands and were allowed to remain in school. The word was that the authorities had based their decision on the "Scriptures." In my view, however, there was nothing scriptural about it. If it is to be believed that all people are created equal, then it seemed to me that racial discrimination in any form had to be a sin. If having sex before marriage was fornication, I could not understand how forbidding students to date members of other races was not discrimination.

During my sophomore year, I attended a Detroit Tigers try-out camp in Lakeland, Florida. During a practice game, I was hit in the head by a pitch and suffered a partially detached retina in my right eye. It was almost a year before I regained most of my vision, and I was not able to play any sport during that year. About that time, my parents were moving back to Birmingham to be closer to family, so I decided to go along and try to make the basketball team at one of the colleges in the city.

Howard College (now Samford University) had a reputation for attracting students with high moral character and providing them with a Christian education, that is, as long as these students were white. Howard was affiliated with the Southern Baptist Convention, and at that time, neither the churches nor the educational institutions were open to blacks. But that was not a major concern to my parents, who were strong Baptists, and besides, all the other colleges in the area were segregated as well. So, with some gentle prodding from my mother, I enrolled in summer school at Howard.

I went to the gym every afternoon and played pickup games with members of the squad to evaluate my prospects. Although Howard competed at a higher level than Cedarville, I matched up well with their players and Walter Barnes, the head basketball coach, heard about me and decided to check me out. By the end of the summer, I was offered a place on the squad. Coach Barnes had an in-depth knowledge of the game and operated under a very different philosophy than either of my coaches at Cedarville. He ran a disciplined half-court offense that consisted of a series of plays designed to get the ball to a specific player. His practices were well-organized and relatively short.

During the early part of the season, I was the first player off the bench at the guard position. I was averaging double figures off the bench when I was promoted to a starting position shortly after Christmas break. I went on to have a very good year and was looking forward to my senior season. We had good returning talent, excellent chemistry, and a great deal of confidence in Coach Barnes. We expected to have another winning season, possibly even upsetting a major college like Auburn or Alabama. But that was not to be. Coach Barnes decided to retire from coaching and go into the insurance business; he was replaced by Virgil Ledbetter, who had been serving as head baseball coach.

Coach Ledbetter was a gifted athlete and a good baseball coach, but in basketball he was completely out of his element. The offensive and defensive systems he installed were out of date and more suited to the game as it was played in the 1940s. My coaches at Cedarville focused on fast breaks while Coach Barnes wanted a moderately paced, well-structured game. To characterize Coach Ledbetter's style, I'd have to say he believed in a physical game, and that's an understatement. As players, we had frequent fights during practice and even once during a pre-game meal. Before a game with Auburn, his instructions made things very clear: "Boys, if we have trouble, I'll go after the coach and you take care of the players." And he meant it.

He also had what I considered an appalling lack of sensitivity for someone who was supposed to be a Christian role model. He was openly contemptuous of anyone who saw things differently than he did. That included fraternity boys, liberals, civil rights activists, and Northerners, to name just a few.

One incident that still sticks out in my mind occurred in November 1963 when we were on our way to Jacksonville to scrimmage Jacksonville State in a final practice game before the start of the season. We heard over the radio that President Kennedy, whom Coach Ledbetter regarded with disdain, had been assassinated in Dallas. "You see that telephone pole on the side of the road?" he asked. "If that pole got struck by lightning, I would care about as much as I do about Kennedy getting killed. I never could stand that S.O.B." Even the players who generally agreed with his views were stunned by his remarks.

Like Pearl Harbor, the Kennedy assassination became a watershed day in history, and people still ask the question: "Where were you when President Kennedy was shot?" Years later I asked one of my friends, a lifelong Republican and no Kennedy admirer, that question. He told me that he was serving on the DMZ in Korea when he got the news and added that he was absolutely devastated. "He was the President and my commander-in-chief," he went on to say. "Whether I agreed with him politically or not was beside the point and I felt our country had suffered a great loss." Those were my sentiments and most likely the sentiments of all of us who heard Coach Ledbetter's comments.

We had numerous altercations with opposing players during the season, including two bench-clearing brawls. The fight during one of our games at Huntingdon College was so bad that it caused the two institutions to sever athletic relations. But it was nothing compared to the one we had at Cumberland. The afternoon before the game, we went back to our motel to rest and watch TV. There wasn't much interesting on the tube, and four of our players decided a few hands of poker would relieve their boredom. Things got out of hand, and somebody put a fist through the wall. The noise brought the manager, who demanded that Coach Ledbetter pay for the damages. He collected from all the players who were involved and paid the rest from his own pocket. Needless to say, nobody was in a very good mood when we took the floor for the game.

Our reputation for combativeness had obviously preceded us, and the fans were spoiling for trouble. During the first half, there was some pushing and shoving, trash talk among the players, and catcalls from the fans, but no fights. About five minutes into the second half, Carl Dunn, our team's "bad boy," committed a hard foul, which led to an exchange of words with the Cumberland player as he walked to the free throw line for two shots. Carl apparently thought it over and decided to take preemptive measures. He punched the player from behind while he was at the free throw line, a cheap shot observed by everyone in the gym except the two officials, who had their backs turned. After a few moments of stunned silence, the Cumberland players and many of the fans came after Carl, and the fight was on. It took the officials and the campus police about five minutes to restore order.

As luck would have it, the Cumberland player missed his second free throw, and the outlet pass came to me. I had made a break at just the right moment and was out ahead of two defenders for what I thought would be an uncontested layup, but my pursuers thought differently: It was payback time. I was in mid-air about to lay the ball against the glass when they hit me from behind, and the last thing I remember is flying through the air. When I came to my senses, I was lying on the floor in front of a stage that was behind the basket. After taking a few minutes to recover, I went back in and played the rest of the game. I did not, however, attempt any more breakaway layups.

As I reflect back on that incident, it occurs to me that we were representing Howard College, a religious institution supposedly made up of students with high moral character, all of us receiving a Christian education. It seems clear that playing poker, trashing motel rooms, and starting fights was not exactly what the Southern Baptist Convention had in mind. But that was only one of the ironies of my playing days at Howard. The others were sanctioned by official policy.

One Saturday night in December we were on a road trip to play William Carey College in Hattiesburg, Mississippi. It was almost dark when we arrived in Hattiesburg about 5:30 P.M. and stopped at a service station to get directions to the college. We got as far as the general area before we got lost again, and by then it had gotten completely dark. Finally, we saw some lights about a half-mile away. As we got closer we saw that the lights seemed to be coming from a fire in a vacant lot. When we got within about fifty yards, we saw a crowd of people wearing white robes gathered around a burning cross. It was a Ku Klux Klan meeting where some guy in a decorated robe was making a speech about how "niggers had to be kept in their place."

We drove on and suddenly found ourselves at the front entrance to William Carey College. I thought about how I was playing basketball for a Southern Baptist college that would not allow blacks to enroll or even let its teams compete against black athletes, and that we were playing another Southern Baptist college with the same racial philosophy. These two "Christian" institutions that taught that "we are all God's children" in their Bible classes were in accord philosophically with the Klan members a few blocks away on one issue: "Niggers had to be kept in their place."

But this was 1963 and I was in the Deep South where white supremacy and segregation were facts of life. Change was still many years away and there was nothing I could do about it. Our season was a big disappointment, and the team struggled much of the time. Coach Ledbetter did his best, but both his lack of basketball knowledge and the combative style of play he encouraged kept our team from reaching its potential. Things probably would have been different if Coach Barnes had remained, but there was nothing I could do about that, either.

Later in life I would come to understand that there was more to Coach Ledbetter than the mean-spirited and inept nature he displayed during those times. He had been thrown into a situation for which he was ill-prepared. Without the skills required, he could only employ the ones he had, which were very useful in training military recruits, leading SWAT teams, modifying the behavior of juvenile troublemakers, and serving in other roles where intimidation and physical force were necessary components of the leadership style. There is some tradition for that style in baseball where the name of Billy Martin comes to mind, but even Bobby Knight, who had some of the same attributes as Coach Ledbetter, along with a great basketball mind, was eventually shown the door. Coach Ledbetter was fired the following year.

The last time I visited with him, he was assistant principal of a high school, doing an outstanding job, and he was more relaxed and happy than I had ever seen him. Without the pressure of coaching in an unfamiliar sport, he seemingly no longer felt the need to cope with his inadequacies by engaging in insensitive and provocative behavior. Shortly after our visit he died unexpectedly. I attended his service where the organist played "Take Me Out to the Ball Game" before the minister gave the eulogy. One of the things I remember most is a large floral spray in the shape of a baseball from his former players. There is something about coaches you play for that becomes part of your life, and over time, I was able to sort through the deck of his shortcomings and find an ace or two that I could keep.

I did have had a very strong senior year in basketball, averaging 14.8 points a game, and that spring I was also undefeated in singles play on our all-victorious tennis team. I was later named ODK Athlete of the Year at Howard. All things considered, I would have to say that I had a good college experience at both Cedarville and Howard. I received a good education and had the opportunity to play three sports at the college level.

Dating back to my experiences at Bucyrus High School, my playing days had taught me all the benefits of working to perfect skills and then learning to mesh with other people on a team. I learned how important the relationship between mind and body had been to me in whatever I had managed to achieve, both on and off the court. It had become clear to me that I wanted a career involved with some aspect of athletics at the college level. I knew that to find employment in that field, I had to earn a graduate degree. With this in mind, I enrolled at the University of Tennessee to pursue a master's degree in health, physical education and recreation.

Sweet Home Alabama

*"Home is the place, that when you go there,
they have to take you in."*
—Robert Frost
In "The Death of the Hired Man."

As I mentioned earlier, images and feelings flow into our minds and evoke a consciousness about where we belong, called by psychologists, a "sense of place." My early childhood in Birmingham, the periodic trips back, and my college experience at Howard created and maintained my own sense of place even though many of those feelings and images, especially in regard to discrimination against blacks, were negative. As I was nearing graduation, one of the most recent images of the state where I was born was Governor George Wallace's famous "Stand in the Schoolhouse Door," an unsuccessful 1963 attempt to prevent a black student from enrolling at the University of Alabama. Even so, a voice from deep inside told me to come home. So even though I had spent my formative years in Ohio, where people's attitudes and beliefs about race were much more like mine, I knew my home was Alabama.

It was while I was in graduate school at Tennessee that I became convinced that my calling in life was to coach and teach student-athletes. I also believed my experience as a player and my academic preparation had given me the knowledge and skills to build winning teams and help mold the character of young athletes. It was with these aspirations in mind that I started looking for coaching opportunities during the spring, even before I finished my studies.

During that spring term I met Willie Shaw, who also wanted to become a coach. Like many of my classmates, he had an impressive background as a college athlete. He had been a NAIA All-American basketball player at Lane College in Jackson, Tennessee. He had been one of the top scorers in the nation and had been invited to try out for the United States Olympic team and survived several cuts before being released from the team. I thought about the many things that Willie and I had in common in terms of family values, playing experiences and life goals. The only real difference between us was skin color. Willie was one of the very few blacks I ever saw at Tennessee and the only one I would have the opportunity to know personally.

We immediately struck up a friendship although we both knew that our association had to be limited to talking to each other between classes or getting together once in a while in his dorm room. The racial climate of the times meant that it would not be prudent for us to do what college students normally do in socializing with their friends, *i.e.*, hanging out together, looking to meet girls and generally having a good time. I regret that I did not press the issue more and take a few risks, for Willie was truly worth knowing. But, unfortunately, I did not and we never became really close friends.

Our lives took amazingly similar paths. We became college basketball coaches, earned doctorates and later served as athletic directors at four-year institutions. Years later I would occasionally see Willie at coaching clinics and meetings. We were always glad to see each other, but it was my perception that we both felt a certain sadness about a friendship that should have been deeper. Even though we both knew that it was just how things were in those times, it did not ease the feeling of melancholy over missing what could have been a closer relationship. As I would discover later, attitudes can change, but then my focus had to be on finding employment in my chosen field.

It was not long before I discovered that having a call is only the beginning. My job search revealed the truth in the familiar proverb that "many are called, but few are chosen." I applied for a number of high school and junior college positions in Alabama, but the schools that made offers didn't provide the right opportunities, and those that seemed promising eventually hired someone else. However, just before I was about to accept a position that I didn't believe I was well suited for, I was invited to interview for coaching jobs at two new junior colleges in Alabama.

The job I had my heart set on was at Patrick Henry Junior College (now Alabama Southern Community College), which was located in Monroeville, Alabama, about ninety miles north of Mobile. It was the hometown of Harper Lee, who had recently published *To Kill a Mockingbird*, a critically acclaimed novel with an enlightened message about racial prejudice, violence, moral tolerance, and dignified courage in the South. The book won the Pulitzer Prize and would become one of the best-loved American novels of the twentieth century. I felt that I had acquitted myself well in the PHJC interview and was elated that my search was close to being over. But close only counts in horseshoes, and several days later I learned I had not been selected. Later, when I learned that their first basketball team only won one game, I decided that things had probably worked out for the best.

In any case, my luck was about to change. Dr. E. R. Knox, president of Northeast State Junior College, located near Scottsboro, Alabama, called me a few days later and asked me to meet him for lunch at the Reid House Hotel in Chattanooga, Tennessee. I remembered the Reid House from my days as a member of the Howard College basketball team because we had stayed there whenever we played the University of Tennessee at Chattanooga. On one occasion, Jimmy Hoffa, who was on trial in the city for labor racketeering, was also a guest. I can remember seeing him get off the elevator one day with several bodyguards.

I went to the interview wearing my best suit and tie, which also happened to be the only suit and tie that I owned at the time. Dr. Knox explained in detail what he was looking for in a coach. He wanted someone who would begin by establishing strong physical education and intramural programs during the first year and then starting a men's basketball program the second year. He also emphasized that he expected his faculty to maintain high standards of ethical and moral conduct; he mentioned specifically that as a single man I would be required to observe proper decorum in my dating relationships with young women on the campus. I assured him that I had both the qualifications and personal attributes he had in mind. Apparently I convinced him, because at the conclusion of the interview he offered me the job. At the age of twenty-three I was about to become the Head Basketball Coach, Athletic Director, Intramural Director and Head of the Department of Health, Physical Education and Recreation at Northeast State Junior College.

The job offer was all the motivation I needed to complete my master's degree, and on Labor Day I set out for Scottsboro to find a place to live. It was about lunch time when I arrived. In those days there were no fast food chain restaurants in small towns in the South, so I decided to check out the Square to find a place to eat. But even if I had been able to locate a café, I would not have been able to get near it because several thousand people were milling around in the Square, and all the parking spaces for several blocks had been taken.

I parked and walked to the Square and could not believe my eyes. Within the confines of a two-block area were all kinds of animals for sale including dogs, horses, mules, goats, sheep, rabbits, coons, fox, sheep, and pigs, along with farm tools and implements, pistols, shotguns, rifles, metal milk cans, clothes, chairs, quilts, and various types of furniture. Vendors were everywhere hawking their wares. There were self-taught musicians of every description, preachers, and politicians at various locations performing or making speeches. I learned that the event was called First Monday. On the first Monday of each month, the people from the surrounding counties bring items to the Square in Scottsboro to sell or trade, and the event held on Labor Day is the biggest one of the year. If my family had not moved to Ohio, I would have learned in eighth-grade Alabama history that Scottsboro is famous for the First Monday tradition.

Scottsboro had another, less appealing claim to fame. The town was the site of the trials of the "Scottsboro Boys," one of the worst and most protracted miscarriages of justice in American history. Even the name of the case symbolizes the racial attitudes and issues of the time period. My reference for the information on this episode was an article written by Douglas Linder entitled "The Scottsboro Boys' Trials." Linder's use of the word "boys" related to the young men who were on trial had nothing to do with the fact that most of the defendants were in their teens. He used the word because in that era, black males, regardless of their age, were routinely called "boys" and that is how the case was referred to in the national media of the day and has been known ever since. On March 25, 1931, nine black youth, ranging in age from twelve to twenty, were "hobo riding" a freight train from Chattanooga, Tennessee, which was headed to Memphis. According to Linder's account, shortly after the train passed into Alabama, a fight broke out between the black boys and a group of white boys. All but one of the white boys were forced off the train near Stevenson, Alabama, where they reported to the station master that the black boys had assaulted two white women who were on the train. Word was sent ahead to Paint Rock, where the train was stopped by an angry mob, and the nine blacks were arrested for assault, roped together, and taken to the Jackson County jail in Scottsboro. Later, one of the women said that she had been raped by six of the boys, and it was assumed that the other woman had been raped by the other three. That night a mob gathered outside the jail, and the governor called in the National Guard to prevent a lynching.

Ten days after their arrest the nine were indicted and arraigned on charges that carried the death penalty. At no point were they asked if they needed the assistance of counsel. On the morning of the trial, a drunken real estate lawyer from Chattanooga with no criminal trial experience offered to assist in representing the defendants. A seventy-year-old local lawyer, who had not tried a case in decades, also said he would help with the defense, and the trial began. Three days later, the first of two boys was found guilty after two hours of jury deliberations. The crowd of thousands outside roared and cheered at the announcement of the verdict. These cheers were heard in the deliberation room and shortly thereafter, the second jury returned the same verdict. Within two weeks all went to trial. One proceeding resulted in a mistrial but in all the others, the defendants were found guilty. With the exception of the twelve-year-old, all received the death penalty.

The case ultimately reached the U.S. Supreme Court, which overturned the convictions; however, before that, there were two more trials. At the third trial, one of the women recanted her testimony and said that none of the boys so much as spoke to her or the other woman, let alone touched them. She went on to testify that the other woman had convinced her to lie to avoid a charge of vagrancy because she was married and did not want her husband to find out that she had left home to work as a prostitute. All the Scottsboro Boys were eventually cleared; nevertheless, they spent many years in jail for a crime that never happened. But all this was before I was born, and I thought surely that people had let go of the racial prejudice that had led to this tragedy. Some had, but as I would later discover, others had not.

Scottsboro is adjacent to Sand Mountain, an Appalachian Plateau about twenty-five miles wide that extends from north Georgia southwest into Alabama for about seventy-five miles to near Gadsden. The ridge includes a number of small communities, including Rainsville, the nearest to Northeast State. Historically the area's culture has been more like that of Appalachia than of the Deep South. Even late into the twentieth century, Sand Mountain maintained customs and traditions that were considerably out of the mainstream of life elsewhere in Alabama. It was an insular society where kinship, shared values and continuity of a way of life mattered greatly and outside influences were not welcome.

Social attitudes were enigmatic in that patterns of behavior that were intuitively contradictory existed side-by-side. The people were very religious and tended to adhere to a very literal interpretation of the Scriptures, some even to the extent of carrying out practices that outsiders view as bizarre. Snake handling is a case in point. While picking up rattlesnakes as part of a worship service was not common on Sand Mountain, neither was it that unusual.

A common thread that ran through almost all religious traditions was that when it comes to sin, there are no shades of gray. Offenses like drinking were to be equally avoided along with things like stealing, committing murder, and other "shalt nots" in the Ten Commandments. On the other hand, it was well-known that on Sand Mountain there were numerous shops that dismantled, retagged, and rebuilt stolen automobiles; that many murders went unsolved; and that bootleg whiskey stills were common.

In 1965 no black people lived in the local towns and there was an unwritten rule that blacks had to be off the mountain by sundown. It was, to say the least, a very creative way of dealing with the commandment that says to love thy neighbor. Apparently someone who couldn't stay overnight wouldn't have been considered a neighbor. While Scottsboro was home to a small black community, the prevailing racial attitude was very similar to that of Sand Mountain.

During my first year on the job, I discovered that although

Sand Mountain and the surrounding area appeared to be peaceful and serene, just beneath the surface was a culture that was hostile and intimidating, especially to outsiders. It was not only one of the most racist areas in the state of Alabama, but it was also home to significant violence, corruption and crime. Many people in law enforcement tended to put their own self interest ahead of public safety.

Each day on my way to work, I drove by a small farm that was owned by a local sheriff. Initially, I was impressed at how immaculately clean and neat the house, barn, and property were. I also noticed that there seemed to be a number of people working at the farm and wondered how he could afford to pay so many on his salary. Later I was told that these farm hands were inmates of the local jails, people who apparently "volunteered" to work for nothing.

As time went by, I learned that corruption among some of the law enforcement officers extended into many other areas, including bootlegging, gang activities, and auto theft. In some cases police and sheriff personnel took payoffs and looked the other way while criminal activities were carried out. In others they were active participants, selling illegal liquor that had been confiscated as "evidence" in raids on bootleggers, collaborating in gang violence, and fencing stolen merchandise.

Another incident a short time later made it clear that local police practiced selective law enforcement, illustrated by a phrase I heard several times: "Select an outsider, a bum, or a nigger and enforce the law." A friend of mine who was a major college head basketball coach called me at work one morning. He told me that he was going to be recruiting in the area and would be staying at the Holiday Inn in Scottsboro that night. He invited me to go out to eat with him. I told him that that sounded great and indicated that I would come by the hotel at 7:00 P.M. to pick him up.

When I arrived at the hotel, the coach was not quite ready and he invited me into his room. Several minutes later, as we were making small talk, there was a knock on the door. When I got up to open it he motioned me back. "Bill, you had better let me get that," he said. "I was involved in an incident earlier today while waiting at a red light and there is no telling who that is." When he opened the door, he was confronted by two Scottsboro police officers with a warrant for his arrest. I was in total shock as they escorted him out of the room, heading for the Scottsboro jail.

I decided to follow them to the jail to see what I could do to help my friend. As I walked in, I noticed that two police officers had a man in custody. He was quite small, maybe five feet, seven inches in height and 130 pounds, drunk and talking incoherently. He was obviously no threat to the two burly policemen. One of the officers told him to shut up, and when the man continued to babble on, I was given a demonstration of Sand Mountain police methods. The officers sprayed him between the eyes with pepper spray, causing him to drop to his knees in agony. "Why did you have to do that?" he asked over and over. The two officers eventually picked the man up by the arms and dragged him into a jail cell.

By this time I was very worried about what might be happening to my friend and asked a young man who was dressed in civilian clothes and sitting behind a desk what I could do. He seemed indifferent to the brutality we both had witnessed and casually handed me some forms to fill out. After I had completed the paper work, he got up and left; about thirty minutes, he came back with my friend, never explaining anything. When he sat back down, we assumed that we were free to go.

On the ride back to the hotel, my friend explained what had happened. He told me that when he first arrived in Scottsboro, a young woman had taken exception to his pulling in front of her at a red light near the square. When he became aware of her irritation, he rolled down his window and tried to explain that he did not see her car and asked her to please excuse his blunder. Unfortunately, his attempt to defuse the situation further enraged the woman and she took down his tag number. We later learned that the woman was close friends with some of the local police officers and used her connections to get a warrant for his arrest. These officers spotted his car at the hotel and got the manager to tell them what room he was in.

What was disturbing about this situation was that my friend was arrested on a trumped-up charge and would probably have spent some time in jail if I had not been with him at the time he was arrested at the hotel. He told me later that he was required to come back to Scottsboro on a later date and face a local judge concerning this matter. The two of us agreed never to say a word to anyone about this situation because if it leaked to the press, there was a chance that he could lose his job.

During the same year, I had another experience that illustrates how pervasive the attitude of racial intolerance was, even by Alabama standards. I was aware from an early age that until the 1960s, segregation was the law and that blacks were not allowed to associate socially with whites. But it didn't normally work the other way, even in Birmingham. Whites who were so inclined could attend black events, patronize black establishments, and even visit black restrooms. Of course, one would have expected to encounter disapproval from some whites (like my mother, for example), but no official sanctions, and most black people didn't care.

One such practice I know went on at movie theaters where whites sat in the lower auditorium and blacks were required to sit in the balcony. As any young kid knew, sitting in the balcony was more fun and the tickets were cheaper. One of my friends told me that during the 1950s he and his buddies always sat in the balcony in his hometown movie theater during Saturday double features and often would see white adults and couples there as well.

Anyway, I was taking a date to the movies in Scottsboro, and we decided it would be fun to sit in the balcony. I didn't anticipate any reaction from the young lady at the ticket booth or certainly nothing more than a raised eyebrow. But that's not how things went. As we walked toward the door that led to the balcony, she stormed out of the booth and blocked our way, almost as if we were about to commit a holdup. "You can't go up there!" she screamed. "Can't you read the sign?"

We were startled, but it hadn't really settled in on either one of us what the problem was. Then I noticed the "Colored Only" sign, but since the Civil Rights Act that had desegregated public facilities had been in effect for several years, I thought maybe it was a relic of the past. "Why not?" I asked the ticket lady. "I thought separate seating was against the law." She then fixed a hateful stare on me and said, "Because we don't care what the federal government says. Hell will freeze over before we let niggers and white people sit together at the movies or any place else in Scottsboro!" she exclaimed.

Over the next few short months, I came to the realization that, in many ways, the prevailing culture in the area seemed to be set in stone, and corruption, racism, and hostility toward anyone that had even a thought of questioning the rules of that closed society were worse than I had thought when I arrived. I would soon discover that things were worse than I could even imagine.

I DID FINALLY GET SOME LUNCH that day on my first visit to Scottsboro, and then I drove around the residential areas to look for a place to live. There were no apartment buildings in town, so my only choice was to rent a room or suite in someone's house. After a few hours I found an upstairs apartment that had a living room, kitchen, and bedroom, along with a private entrance. After reaching a verbal agreement with the owner of the house, I moved in my belongings. This did not take long because everything that I owned was in my car.

The next morning I left for work, never having seen the campus or even knowing exactly where it was located. When I asked for directions at a general store and gas station, all I got from the attendant was a puzzled look. He said he had never heard of a college in the area. I told him it was on Sand Mountain near Rainsville, and I could tell by his expression that something was registering. "You know, I saw what looked like a new building under construction several miles this side of Rainsville on Highway 35," he said. With these vague directions in mind, I headed across the B.B. Comer Bridge that spanned Guntersville Lake and started the three-mile drive up Highway 35 to the top of Sand Mountain. Once I reached the top, I went through the tiny village of Section and drove about six more miles through Duncan's Crossroads. Then I looked out into a field and saw several nearly completed one-story buildings.

"This can't be it," I thought to myself. The buildings were located about a hundred yards off the road. I drove up an unfinished drive that went through the corn field and parked my car in a small parking lot beside a few other vehicles. I went in the main door of the nearest building to ask for further directions. Once inside, I walked into an office area and saw a lady sitting by the desk. Before I could say anything, she told me her name was Emma Lou Lovelady and offered her assistance. "I'm Bill Elder and I'm looking for Northeast State Junior College," I said. "You must be our physical education teacher and coach," she responded with a friendly smile. "Dr. Knox has told me about you. Please go next door to classroom 103. We'll have our first meeting of the morning in there. It's good to have you aboard."

It was 8:57 A.M. when I took my seat in room 103 for the meeting. The acoustical tile had not been installed, the roof was visible through the rafters, and there was electrical conduit dangling from the ceiling. There were about twenty people in the room and I was evidently the last one to arrive. I had just taken my seat when Dr. Knox made his entrance. "I would like to welcome you, the first faculty and staff, to Northeast State Junior College," he announced.

After about an hour's talk, mostly about Dr. Knox's vision for the college, we were told where our office were and instructed to go there and spend the rest of the morning settling in. I was told that my office was located in a small building located across a narrow road that ran through the middle of the site. The building didn't look very impressive, but once inside I was pleasantly surprised. There was a varsity dressing room, men's and women's dressing rooms with showers, and an office. All things considered, the building was quite acceptable, and even though the office was small, since I had never had one before, there would be no complaining from me.

I had forgotten the time of our scheduled afternoon meeting and decided to call Mrs. Lovelady, whom I had learned was Dr. Knox's secretary. I dialed the college's main number but kept getting a strange sounding busy signal. After seven or eight more attempts to make the call to the Administration Building, I finally decided just to walk over and ask her. When I told Mrs. Lovelady that I had not been able to get her on the phone, she started laughing. "I'm sorry," she said. "I thought that Dr. Knox mentioned in our first faculty meeting that it is a long distance call from your office to the administration building. That road you crossed is the county line. The Administration Building is in Jackson County and your office is in DeKalb County." I would learn later that in determining where junior colleges would be located, the rule was politics first, education second, and Northeast State was no exception.

At the afternoon meeting we were told to work on our lesson plans and get ready for the start of classes the following week. The problem was that all I had was a building with an office and shower facilities in the middle of a field. There was no gymnasium nor were there any outdoor facilities for physical education activities. There was also the question of what to do during inclement weather, but I decided I would figure out a way to cross that bridge when I came to it.

The next day I met Claude Dilbeck, the maintenance director. I mention his name because if not for his good efforts, there would not have been any physical education program at all that first semester. In the course of my life there have been times when I've had a problem that seemed insurmountable, and someone would suddenly appear and "fix" things. Typically these people have had nothing to gain, nor have they expected anything in return. They met my needs simply out of the goodness of their hearts. A friend of mine calls these people "kind strangers." Others say they follow the example from one of Christ's parables and suggest they are "Good Samaritans." When I think of those who have helped me in that way, the name of Claude Dilbeck always comes to mind.

He located someone with a front-end loader who leveled the ground near my office for three outdoor volleyball courts and two touch football fields and also moved a mound of dirt about eight feet high and forty feet long so that I could teach an archery class. He said he would not be able to have grass planted in time for the start of school, but I was more than happy with what he had accomplished in a very short time, and grass was the farthest thing from my mind.

My next job was to order the equipment which consisted of volleyballs, nets, footballs, scrimmage vests, bows and arrows, and the like. Dr. Knox let me order the equipment from one of the Huntsville sporting good stores that guaranteed it would be in place by the beginning of classes. So in less than one week, I had everything in place for the initiation of the physical education program at Northeast State Junior College. It was not exactly the program that Dr. Knox had envisioned, but it was better than anything I had thought possible only a few days earlier.

With a physical education program underway, I was ready to turn my attention to building a basketball program for the following year. I knew that having a team would provide students gifted with athletic ability an opportunity to excel in competitive sports against like institutions. It would also serve as a means by which other students, faculty, staff, and eventually, alumni could be brought together in support of a common rallying point to generate school spirit and round

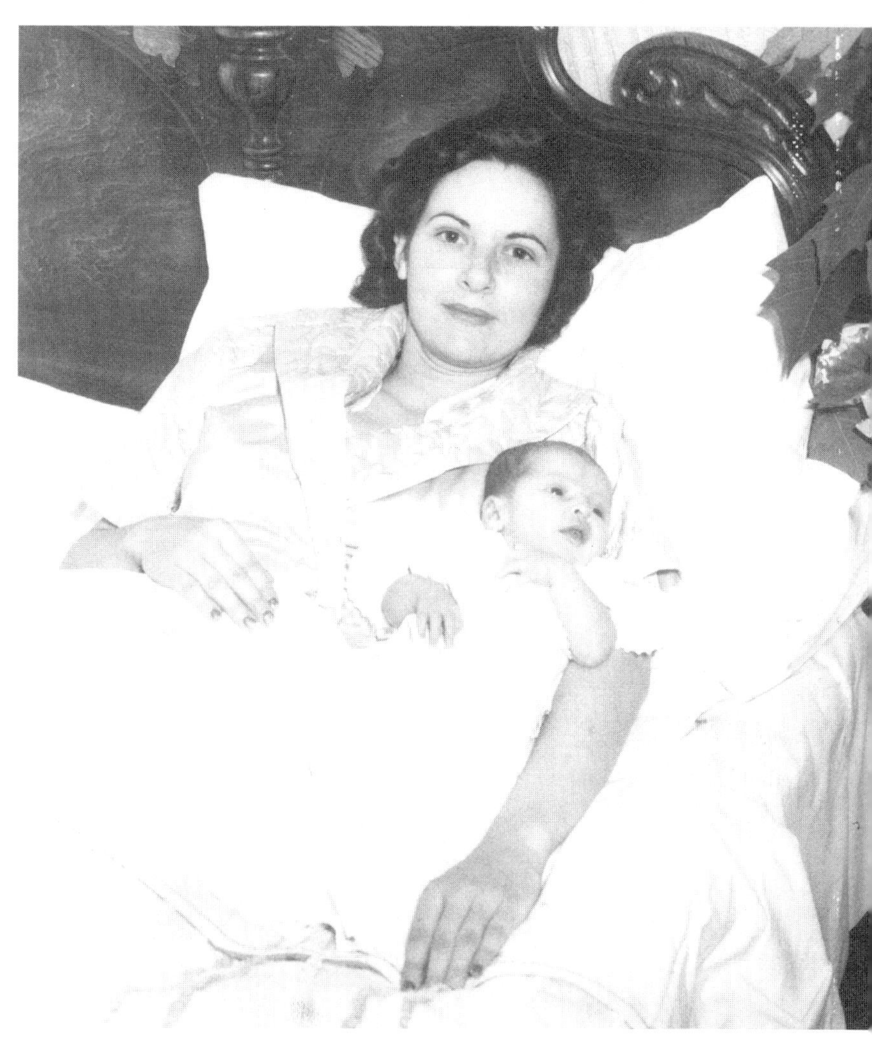

Elder with his mother, Laura Elizabeth Elder, shortly after
his birth in Birmingham, Alabama.

(Photographs courtesy of the author)

Above, Elder gives his best football "tough guy" look for the Bucyrus High School photographer. Below, Elder (left) gets last-minute instructions at Municipal Stadium for a try-out with the Cleveland Indians.

Elder passes and cuts during a Howard College [now Samford University] basketball game against Auburn University at the Sports Arena in Auburn.

Howard College's 1963–64 undefeated tennis squad. Elder is standing, second from left.

Opposite Page: Top, the inaugural Northeast State Junior College faculty and staff. Bottom, the Northeast State Junior College campus as it looked in the late 1960s.

Above, the Mustangs were Alabama Junior College State Champions for the 1966–67 season. Below, James Edwards (14), Elder, and Ken Wilson (10) hold some of the loot after winning the 1966–67 Alabama Junior College State Championship.

Northeast, Calhoun Advance To Finals

BY HERBY KIRBY
Post-Herald Sports Writer

Northern Division runner-up Northeast Alabama stunned Southern Division champion George C. Wallace 92-70 in the opening game of the Alabama State Junior College Basketball Tournament at Samford University last night.

John C. Calhoun, the Northern Division champion, defeated Enterprise 86-68 to make it an all-Northern Division finals.

Enterprise, the No. 2 team in the Southern, will meet the Wallace Governors at 7 tonight, preceding the championship game between Calhoun and Northeast.

Ken Wilson, a slim, 6-3 forward, threw in 27 points to pace Northeast in its victory over George C. Wallace.

Wilson had the soft touch that enabled him to be the difference between winning and losing.

Larry Lingerfelt had 22 points to be a big help to the victorious Mustangs, and Larry Smith chimed in with 17 points.

Bruce Travick hit on a 15-foot jump shot to give Wallace a 2-0 lead as the game started. But it was the Governors' last lead. Wilson hit seven consecutive points to run Northeast's lead to 11-4.

The Governors came back and caught up at 29-29 but never moved out in front.

The Mustangs led 42-35 at the half and put the game out of reach outscoring the Dothan team 14-3 during the early stages of the second half.

Bob Pope with 21 points and John Tomlinson with 18 were the top gunners for Calhoun's Warhawks as they sped up after a sluggish start and breezed by Enterprise's Bollweevils.

Terry Smith of Enterprise was high scorer with 27 points, even though he spent a good deal of the time on the bench, having been pulled by his coach twice after a display of temper had caused a technical foul to be called on him.

The Bollweevils jumped out to a 11-4 lead as Smith hit on four jumpers and two free throws.

After Smith was pulled a first time, the Warhawks scored 10 consecutive points to assume the lead, never to relinquish it.

* * *

NORTHEAST (92)—Lingerfelt 24, Bell 2, Pack 6, Wilson 27, Garrett 8, Edwards 13, Fanning 2, Picket 10.
WALLACE (70)—Kennedy 5, Sconvers 4, Bryson 10, Houston 15, Smith 17, Rodgers 3, Shelley 2, Singlecary 8, Travick 6.

Northeast	42	50—92
Wallace	35	35—70

* * *

CALHOUN (86) — Harris 14, Pope 21, Woodall 11, Campbell 13, Tomlinson 18, Smith 2, Lee 3, Turpin 2, Livingston 2.
ENTERPRISE (68) — Smith 27, P. Kelly 6, E. Kelly 4, Carnly 4, Bowdon 6, Lewis 6, Brown 7, Cordie 8.
Halftime — Calhoun 35, Enterprise 27.

Engagement photo of Bill Elder's better half, Vivian Logan Elder.

NJC Is Second State Champs

SECTION -- The Northeast State Junior College Mustangs won the Alabama Junior College State Championship by defeating Calhoun Technical Junior College 56-38.

The Mustangs reached the finals by beating George C. Wallace Junior College of Dothan 92-70 while Calhoun beat Enterprise Junior College 86-68 to enter the finals.

Northeast was led by the second half scoring of James Edwards. Edwards scored 17 of his 21 points in the second half. Edwards was given strong support by Bruce Pickett who tallied 12 points. Larry Lingerfelt led the Mustangs in rebounding while David Pack, Kenneth Wilson, and Phil Garrett were outstanding on defense.

Coach Bill Elder contributed the Mustangs success to a disciplined offensive attack, a tight defense and an all out effort on the part of each player.

Kenneth Wilson and Larry Lingerfelt were named to the all Tournament Team.

Northeast concluded their first year in intercollegiate basketball with a 15 win 6 lose record. The Mustangs won their last 9 games in a row.

Local newspaper coverage of the Mustangs' first Alabama Junior College State championship.

Above, Northeast State Junior College 1970–71 basketball team. Below, Alabama Junior College Northern Division Co-champions and Alabama Junior College State Tournament Semi-Finalists (1971–72).

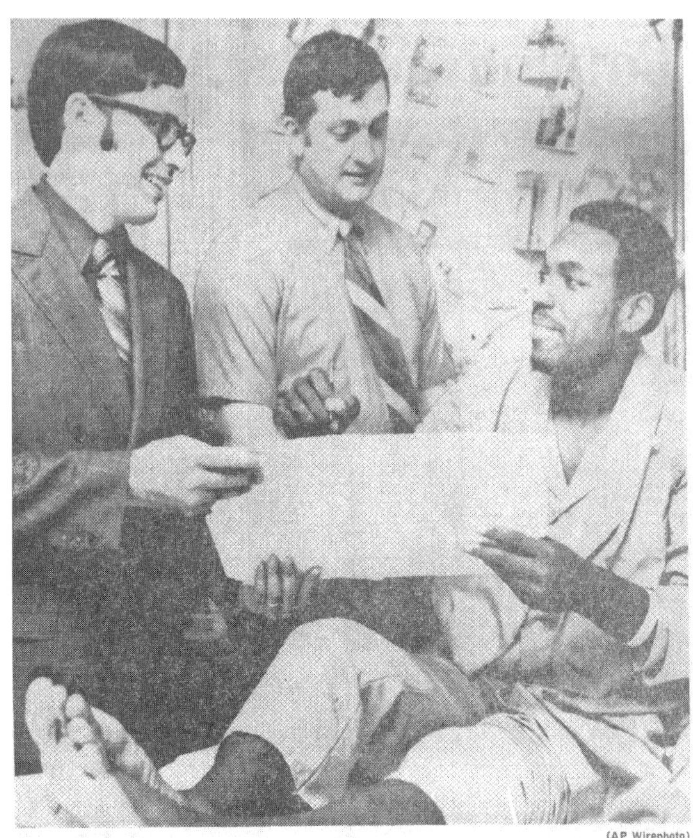

CRAYTON GETS GRANT-IN-AID FROM NORTHEAST STATE
... Elder (C), Jim Phifer Watch (See Easterling Column)

Studies in Courage Come In All Colors

Elder awards Lebron Crayton a basketball scholarship the night before Crayton was to have his leg amputated.

Charles Jackson (30) goes up and over opponents as Jack Newton looks on.

Elder gives the Mustangs coaching instructions.

Opposite Page: Charles
Jackson takes a short
jumper as Charlie
Patton (22) and Ron
West get in position for
an offensive rebound.

Steve Easley (44) pulls up and fires from the wing.

Charles Jackson, left, and Dean Breeden clown for a photographer during a break in a practice.

Bill Elder, in retirement in 2006.

out the creation of a typical college campus setting. Hopefully, a team would also generate community involvement and give local citizens a stake in the success of the institution, both in sports and academics. Now all I needed to do was recruit some student athletes, teach them the fundamentals of college basketball, and find a place to play.

They Called Me Coach

"I get to coach. I know I've been blessed."
—JIM VALVANO
Longtime basketball coach, North Carolina State University

With my physical education program well underway, I was able to turn my attention to recruiting players who, during the following season, would become the first basketball team at Northeast State. I knew that north Alabama was a hotbed of basketball, similar to many rural areas in the Midwest. With this in mind, I decided to recruit mostly local players. I had heard that Sylvania High School, located about five miles from the campus, had a six-feet, three-inch forward who was considered one of the better players on Sand Mountain. After watching David Pack play, I decided that I wanted to make him my first signee. I met with David and his coach at the high school and he seemed delighted with the idea of playing at Northeast State. I told him that I would meet him at his home the following Saturday to make it official.

Even though it was only a short distance to his home from the college, I decided to check out a state car to make the signing more official. In those days, each state junior college had a small fleet of state cars for business use by its employees. All of the state cars were the same. Each one was a green Chevrolet with the Seal of Alabama on the front doors. I got the keys to the car on Friday afternoon and picked it up from the parking lot at 1:00 P.M. on Saturday. Although I had directions to David's house, I wanted to give myself plenty of time to get there by 2:00 P.M. when we had scheduled a signing ceremony with David and his parents. My decision to get an early start was a good one because after driving around the Sylvania community area for about a half hour, I was hopelessly lost. I finally stopped at one of the many general stores that I had seen to try to get better directions.

These stores were pretty much alike. They were wooden structures with two gas pumps in the front, groceries and soft drinks inside, and living quarters in back for the owner. On the front porch there were usually several men in bib overalls playing dominoes or just sitting around shooting the breeze. I parked my car at the front of such a store and asked one of the men on the porch if he knew where David Pack lived. He squinted his eyes and thought long and hard. "I don't think I've ever heard of a family around here by the name of Pack," he said, shaking his head. "You must be in the wrong county," he added helpfully. After stopping at several more stores and getting about the same answer, I was pretty discouraged. Finally, a local teenager tapped me on the shoulder as I was getting into the car. "You know what your problem is, don't you?" he asked in a low voice. I assured him that I had no idea what my problem was. "David Pack is a basketball star. You would think that most people would have heard of him and at least somebody would know where he lives," I said in exasperation. "You're not from around here, are you?" he asked with a knowing smile on his face. "No, I'm not," I answered. "I just moved here from Birmingham and I'm the new basketball coach at Northeast State Junior College. I was supposed to sign David to a basketball scholarship about five minutes ago."

I could tell from his expression that he had figured out the problem. He told me that I was in a dry county, and many of the local farmers operated stills to supplement their incomes and that people who showed up in state cars, wearing suits, and asking a lot of questions, were usually from the Alabama Department of Revenue (in local parlance, "revenuers"). He explained that the people I had talked to obviously thought I was looking for the Packs so I could arrest them for making moonshine whiskey. Fortunately, however, he had seen my picture in the *Sand Mountain Reporter* and knew who I was. He gave me directions and I arrived shortly at the Pack's house, only about ten minutes late.

The house had weathered wood siding that was probably white at one time but had not likely seen a fresh coat of paint in at least twenty-five years. The front steps were made of cinder blocks. The yard was bare ground and appeared to have been recently swept with a brush broom. Two mixed-breed dogs dozed on the front porch. They opened their eyes briefly to check me out when I knocked on the door but were apparently not impressed because they both went back to sleep.

David's mother met me at the door. She was probably in her forties and was attractive, wearing a plain dress that was clean and well pressed, very much the image of a farm wife in a Norman Rockwell painting. I introduced myself and she went to get David who was out in the field working with his father. I had a seat on the living room sofa, which was covered by a blanket. The other furniture in the room looked worn, but the house appeared to be well-kept. It appeared that the

Packs were like most farm families of that day who did not have a large income but would not be considered poor because they raised most of their own food and managed well on their limited resources.

After the mother left to get David, a young boy and girl came into the living room and stood in front of the sofa and stared at me. The boy appeared to be about three years old and the girl, a year or so younger. "Hello, my name is Bill," I said, "and what are your names?" Neither of them said a word, just stood there staring until David and his mother came through the front door. David was barefooted and was not wearing a shirt.

His mother suggested that we go into the kitchen and sit at the table. She served iced tea and I talked to them about how we planned to have a basketball team the following year in the Northern Division of the newly formed Alabama Junior College Conference. I told her that the scholarship would cover David's tuition, books, and fees and that he would have to live at home since we did not have any dormitories. I told her that the junior college was accredited and his credits would transfer to any four-year college that he wanted to attend. I assured her that we would put academics first, that David would be expected to take a full load of sixteen credit hours, and that we would do our best to ensure that he graduated with the AA degree at the end of his two years so that he could transfer to a four-year school as a junior.

Mrs. Pack listened very carefully. "David is the first person in our family to go to college," she said. "We have brought him up right and you should have no problems with him. If you do, all you have to do is call me and we will straighten him out immediately. All we ask of you is to treat him fairly.

I am mainly interested in what he does in the classroom. The basketball will take care of itself. I just want him to have the opportunity to have a better life than my husband and I have had," she continued, looking David straight in the eye. "Now where do we sign?" she asked, indicating that our meeting was over. "David needs to get back to work." I got the contract out of the folder that I was carrying, and we all signed in the designated areas, and without any fanfare David became the first signee in the history of the Northeast State Junior College basketball program.

Scottsboro and Pisgah high schools, the latter located near-by on Sand Mountain, also had excellent basketball programs. Although I lived in Scottsboro, there were several reasons I decided to focus my recruiting efforts on Pisgah, at least for the first year. They were the current state champions in their division and many players from that school had gone on to play in college, including Bill McGriff and Wallace Tinker, who had played on an SEC championship team at Auburn University. Another reason was that their coach, Paul Cooley, had the kind of flexible, team-oriented approach that I planned to use. Coach Cooley reminded me of Jim Valvano. He wore a coat and tie and always looked impeccable although he was usually in a frenzied state during games, jumping up and down and yelling instructions, corrections, and encouragements from the sideline. His teams responded by making adjustments during the game and switching styles of play according to what the situation dictated.

Also, Pisgah was a country school and I felt that boys who grew up in rural areas would have been raised like David Pack, with good morals, a strong work ethic, respect for authority, and other attributes I wanted in my players. A final reason I decided to pass on Scottsboro was that even though they were in a higher classification, Pisgah was one of their bitter rivals. It was going to be difficult enough that first year without dealing with the possible distraction of players having lingering hard feelings against each other.

I knew that I could not get the best players from Pisgah to come to a first-year program and a new junior college. I decided, therefore, to go after their fourth- and fifth-best starters, Ken Wilson and James Edwards, and their top substitute, Bruce Pickett. Ken and James, like David Pack, were from families with limited means. Ken's dad was disabled from an automobile accident and James's family ran a tiny general store in Rosalie, a small community close to Pisgah. His cousin Bruce, whose father was a rural mail carrier, would be the only player on my team whose family was remotely close to being considered middle class. I signed these three players one afternoon in Coach Cooley's office at Pisgah High School.

Several days later I signed Larry Lingerfelt from Valley Head High School. Valley Head was a small community in the valley between Sand Mountain and Lookout Mountain. Larry had played on a mediocre team but was a great leaper and rebounder. Finally, I signed Phil Garrett, a center from Albertville High School. At six feet, six inches, he was the only player on the squad who stood above six feet, three inches. He was not very mobile but had a reasonably good shooting touch. We needed a big man under the basket and he would prove valuable as the season progressed.

I had recruited a squad of thirteen players, and none were black. Although by that time all public institutions in Alabama were required to comply with the Civil Rights Act and the U.S. Justice Department had recently blocked the attempt by

Governor Wallace to prevent black students from enrolling at the University of Alabama, segregation in most parts of Alabama was still very much a fact of life. This was especially true in northeast Alabama. Blacks were not only excluded from "white" schools, restaurants, theaters, and other public accommodations, they were not even permitted to live on Sand Mountain.

As I pointed out earlier, this was an unwritten rule, but there were towns in the area where the message was not quite as subtle. For example in the recent past, Cullman, which was less than fifty miles away, had posted a sign at the city limits warning black people to be out by sundown. While all this chafed against my sense of right and wrong, it was clear to me that any action on my part to recruit black players under these circumstances would be an exercise in futility. I felt that my chances of bringing about change would be greatly improved after I had established myself as a coach and built a winning program, so I decided to face that issue at a later time.

There were still many things to be done before I could even begin my coaching duties. I ordered home and road game uniforms, game warm-ups, practice uniforms, basketballs, towels, and other necessities, but I still did not have a place to practice and play. I worked out a deal with the principal at Section High School, located in a small town about four miles west of our new campus. Although Section was only a country crossroads, a local booster had donated the money to build a well-equipped gym with an excellent floor and 3,000 permanent bleacher seats, better at that time than many major colleges' facilities, including the Sports Arena at Auburn and Foster Auditorium at Alabama. It seemed to be an ideal arrangement. But again, things are not always what they seem.

One of the stipulations made by the administration was that we could not ask anyone to leave the gym while we were practicing. We were also told that we could not ask anyone to be quiet, no matter how loud they became. As anyone who has ever coached would know, this was a big problem. Most coaches want their players to be quiet and pay close attention when they are talking. But, as the saying goes, "beggars can't be choosers." I explained the situation to our players and told them that it could work out for the best for us in the long run. I told them that every practice would be like a game on the road where the fans would be making a lot of noise to distract them, and they could gain valuable experience facing the hostile atmosphere of enemy territory.

It got to the point at practice that it was almost like nobody else was even there. One day two high school students who were in the gym while they were waiting for their school bus got into a fight. Our players did not even stop to look, just went on with their work. At some point the principal came in and broke up the fight, but it had no effect on our practice. It was like there was an invisible wall from the front edge of the bleachers on both sides of the floor to the roof. As I had hoped, the team went on to play as well or better on the road than we did at home.

We started practice for the inaugural basketball season on the first of October. Given the fact that I was head coach of a college team at the age of twenty-three (twenty-four by the start of my second year) and had no prior coaching experi-ence, I went into the season expecting to have my authority as a coach challenged by some of my players. I was not ready, however, for this challenge to occur as soon as it did. After practice on Friday of our first week, I met with the team in the dressing room to review practice and make some announcements. I concluded my talk by saying that I would see them at 10:00 A.M. on Saturday. Since I did not have an office at the Section High School gym, I usually went back out to the gym and sat in the bleachers to be available to any of the players who wanted to talk with me.

After sitting there for about five minutes, one of my players who had become a late addition to our squad when I signed him to a scholarship a few days prior to the opening of the 1966–67 academic year came up and sat down next to me. This young man had been a big star at one of the local high schools and was one of the most talented players on the squad. His "me first" attitude, however, had become quickly obvious and had carried over to our practice sessions. I could see that it was going to have an effect on the morale of the team. His teammates developed a slogan about him: he never saw a shot that he didn't think he could make. I had already had a few run-ins with him related to his shot selection. As he walked toward me that afternoon, I thought perhaps he wanted to discuss this with me. "Coach, I won't be at practice on Saturday," he announced, matter-of-factly. I asked him to explain why he needed to miss practice, thinking that if there was a good reason, I would excuse him. From his expression I could tell that he was becoming annoyed. The idea that informing me was not enough, that he was actually supposed to ask permission to miss practice, clearly did not sit well with him. "I have other plans," he said. "I'm not coming to practice."

I could not believe what I was hearing. I would never have talked to one of my coaches like that. It was beyond my comprehension that a player who had practiced for only a few days would be so disrespectful. I thought maybe I could make him understand that this was not the way things worked, at least not with me. "Let's start over again," I said. "It is unacceptable to tell me you will not be at practice without giving me a reason." He merely repeated what he had said before. At this point, my patience was starting to wear thin. Choosing my words carefully, I gave him an ultimatum: "Let me make this clear; you have two choices: you can show up for practice on Saturday and remain on the team or you can miss practice and be dismissed," I said.

"I won't be there," he replied, "so I guess the ball is in your court." With this parting shot, he walked down the bleachers and left.

It came as not surprise to me that the cocky young player was absent on Saturday, and then showed up for our next practice on Monday. This was what I had expected, and I was waiting for him at the dressing room door. As he came down the hallway to the dressing room, I stopped him and said, "As you will remember, I gave you two choices on Friday. You made the choice to miss practice without permission. Turn in your practice equipment to the manager because you are no longer a member of the team." He looked stunned for a moment, and then without saying a word, he walked into the dressing room, turned in his equipment, and left.

After my confrontation with this could-have-been star player, I went out to wait on the bleachers as the team got ready to work out. Our manager, Tony Townsen, came out of the dressing room and climbed up to where I was sitting. "Did you kick someone off the team?" he asked incredulously. "One of the guys just gave me his equipment and stormed out of the dressing room, slamming the door behind him. He was really mad." I explained that I had given the now-former Mustang two choices and that it was more a matter of his kicking himself off the team. Tony worried that some of his friends on the team might also quit in protest of my actions. It occurred to me that there could be other consequences as well. I knew that Sand Mountain was a tight-knit community and that the principal at Section High School might take exception to what I had done. It was not out of the question that he might tell us to find another place to practice and play games in, especially if a significant number of local players quit the squad. I remember taking a deep breath as I thought through what my next steps should be.

After everyone was dressed and getting in the gym ready to practice, I sent them back to the dressing room so that we could have a team meeting in private. I knew that this was only the first of many hard decisions that I would have to explain if I was going to be a career coach. I felt it was my responsibility as the head coach to teach my players "life skills" through the everyday situations that came up. I also thought it was important to explain to them that the basis for my decisions was not just my opinion, but what the Scriptures taught regarding respect for authority and putting the welfare of others ahead of satisfying personal desires.

When I walked into the dressing room, the team members had already taken their seats in front of their lockers. I could tell by the looks on their faces that word had spread about their teammate's dismissal from the team. I began by saying, "I want you to know up front that I am the type of person who deals with things directly. As you get to know me, you will learn that I will be truthful with you. You will also learn that I am not one to let problems linger. As most of you know, I dismissed one of your teammates from the squad." I then told them the basis for my decision: that in all life situations, someone is in charge and that authority has to be respected, that accomplishing the objective is the first priority, and that people working together as a group could accomplish much more than could individuals pursuing their own selfish interests. I concluded the meeting by saying, "This will be the last time I address this issue in one of our meetings, but I will be glad to talk about it with any of you individually. Now, let's hit the floor and get to work."

It was my first major decision as a coach, and despite the fact that I did not know how things were going to turn out, I felt at peace with it. I felt that dismissing this player would be the best thing in the long run for our team and also for player himself. The biggest reason for my sense of peace was that, in my opinion, I had made my decision based on sound Christian principles. The following morning several of the key players on the team came by my office and told me that they supported my decision. And to my considerable relief, there were no repercussions from anyone at Section High School. In retrospect, I believe that both the principal and the coach at the high school, being very familiar with the players in the community, realized that the failure of the player to adjust to the virtues of discipline and teamwork had cost him the opportunity to play college basketball. To my knowledge, no blame was ever leveled at me.

Our first game during that inaugural season was at home with Calhoun State Junior College. I had played college basketball at two institutions and had been exposed to the philosophies and styles of four different coaches. I never went through a practice session or played in a game without learning something. My graduate studies had prepared me to deal with both the physical and psychological aspects of athletics. All that and (in those days) a dime would get you a cup of coffee. The real question was, could I take a group of country boys from Sand Mountain who were, for the most part, average players and substitutes on their high school squads, and make them into a winning college basketball team? I was about to find out.

Calhoun State started the game in a straight man-to-man defense and we got out to a lead. Then their veteran coach, Bob Shuttlesworth, changed to a 1-2-2 zone defense. I had seen this defense before and we had practiced against it so I knew what we needed to do. The problem was, he had only disguised his defense to make it appear they were playing a 1-2-2 zone so that I would adjust our offense to attack it. So I called time-out and did exactly what he hoped I would do. When it didn't work, I tried several more offensive sets and they didn't work either. Calhoun State was using what was known as a "drop zone" but by the time I figured that out, it was too late. They had built a double digit lead and went on to win the game by a score of 70-57. After the game Coach Shuttlesworth shook my hand and complimented our team on their good effort. I could tell by his expression that what he was thinking was, "I just gave this rookie a lesson in coaching." And his sentiments were accurate. Our team of average high school players and substitutes did exactly what I asked of them. The fact that they lost the game was totally my fault.

I was honest with our players after the game, telling them that I had not prepared them for the drop zone. I told them that I took complete responsibility for the loss. I also told them that I would not ever let this happen again. It was another in a long line of blessings in disguise for me. First of all, it taught me that I did not know as much basketball as I thought I did. It also taught me that if I was going to be successful in this profession, I had to be prepared for the unexpected.

We struggled at first and twelve games into the season, our record was 6-6. Things started to fall into place at this point, and we finished the regular season by winning seven games in a row and placing second in our division, which qualified us for a berth in the Alabama Junior College State Tournament. As luck would have it, the tournament was held at Howard College in the same arena that I had played in several years earlier.

We beat George C. Wallace of Dothan 92-70 in the first round of the tournament and advanced to the championship game, along with Calhoun State, who defeated Enterprise Junior College 86-68. We were definitely looking forward to playing Calhoun again to get revenge for the beating we had taken from them in our first game of the season. To say that we were prepared for their drop zone would have been an understatement. We won by 56-38 to take the state championship and cap off the first basketball season in the history of Northeast State Junior College with a storybook ending. When I met Coach Shuttlesworth after the game, I tried to be as gracious to him as he had been to me after beating us at our opening game and then choosing not to gloat over teaching me a lesson. The fact that we went from losing by 13 to winning by 18 was never mentioned. He understood that the numbers meant I had learned my lesson well.

By the end of my third year, my teams had a cumulative record of 53 wins against 22 losses. The Mustangs had won one state championship and been runners-up another year as well as being named the number one defensive team in the state three years running. I felt I had established myself as a coach. On the other hand, I still had not recruited a single black player.

I remembered three years previously when I had reflected on my first all-white recruiting class. My thought then was to bring in black players "when I had established myself and built a winning program." It is human nature to put off doing the right thing until a more opportune time, and then when that time arrives, to put it off again when things will be even better. Maybe it's like cleaning out a closet, quitting smoking, writing a thank-you note, studying for an exam, or even making spiritual decisions in our lives. I was reminded of a passage in Luke in which Christ expressed His displeasure when a disciple wanted to put off following Him until he could bury his father.

I would like to think I was prepared to do the right thing on my own, but I'll never know. It was during my fourth year at Northeast State that Dr. Knox called me into his office to discuss an important matter. He invited me to sit down, looked me in the eye, and got straight to the point: "Coach Elder, I need you to help us desegregate the student body and athletic teams. As you know, we have a minimal amount of black students on campus but we need to become more integrated. I want you immediately to begin recruiting black basketball players. You will have my full support." I was surprised at the unequivocal language of Dr. Knox's commitment to fully integrate the school and his directive to me to move forward expeditiously in carrying out his intentions. It made me wonder if his directive was related to "doing the right thing" or if it was for another reason.

IN MANY CITIES AND TOWNS in Alabama, there is a statue of a Confederate soldier honoring the bravery of Southern men who were willing to follow the orders of their officers to march into battle to fight, and if necessary, die for "The Cause." This tradition is often invoked when one is given a difficult assignment, and the scene that comes to my mind now about my time in Dr. Knox's office that day is Pickett's famous charge on the third day of the Battle of Gettysburg. It was there that a division left the cover of a forest and advanced across an open field in an attempt to capture Cemetery Ridge. The troops were decimated by rifle and cannon fire from heavily fortified Union positions and forced to retreat. History records Pickett's charge as one of the finest examples of the courage of soldiers under fire. History also records that many of the senior officers stayed back in the forest. They knew that the charge had little chance of succeeding and that most of the men would be killed or wounded. Fighting and dying for The Cause was fine as long as it was done by somebody else. I would soon come to understand that in the cause of equal opportunity at Northeast State Junior College, that somebody else was me.

A Charge To Keep

"He was a straight-A student; he was a very physical player, an excellent rebounder, and I felt like he could help our basketball team."

—**Roy Skinner**

Head basketball coach, Vanderbilt University, on why he signed Perry Wallace, the first black player in the SEC

A charge to keep I have, a God to glorify" are lines from a Methodist hymn, written as a call to recruit people to follow Christ. There is nothing in the hymn that suggests where they should play college basketball. On the other hand, I believed that God wanted all people to have the opportunity to go as far as their hard work and talent would take them. I also believed that in opening the basketball program at Northeast State to black players, I would be carrying out His will the same way that Roy Skinner had done at Vanderbilt three years previously. Scottsboro was only about a hundred and fifty miles from Nashville, but in terms of people's attitudes and beliefs about race and their readiness to accept change, it might as well have been in another country.

I have often wondered if Dr. Knox's decision to actively desegregate the student body and the athletic program was due to a sudden epiphany that revealed to him that he should follow the right moral course or if it might have something to do with the possible loss of federal funding for the institution. Northeast State, to my knowledge, had the fewest black students of any public junior college in the state of Alabama. In my way of thinking, Dr. Knox's plan was evidently to use me as the major source of recruitment of black students. It things went badly, I would take the blame. On the remote chance that the effort succeeded, he could, of course take the credit. Since only God knows what is in the heart of a man, I chose to assume that Dr. Knox's intentions were honorable.

In retrospect, however, there were warning flags that the directive might not have been made in good faith. The word around campus was that we had a significant number of administrators and faculty who were not in support of integration. The rumor mill had it that one individual was a member of the Ku Klux Klan and had even had Klan meetings on his property. I knew also that we had some University of Mississippi alumni on our faculty and staff. I often wondered if they believed that the rioters had been justified in attempting to uphold the principle of state's rights when James Meredith became the first black to enroll in that institution.

A friend of mine from Alabama was serving in the 82nd Airborne Division at Ft. Bragg, North Carolina, during this time. He told me that he was dismayed that the Division which, historically, had been involved in such a noble action as leading the invasion on D-Day to liberate Europe from oppression, was being sent to Oxford because our own citizens were being oppressed. I also learned that Ross Barnett, the governor of Mississippi, had had a large role in instigating the demonstrations in order to provoke a confrontation. The violence at Ole Miss established a pattern that was repeated in Birmingham, Selma, Tuscaloosa, and other locations in the Deep South where officials would blame the federal government and "outside agitators" for creating the race issue and publicly express "fears" that any move to provide equal rights would cause whites to rise up and defend their way of life. For some, this was all they needed to hear to converge on whatever location where their services were needed to make these fears into a self-fulfilling prophecy.

Despite my misgivings and sense of foreboding, I was in favor of the desegregation initiative. First, it was the right thing to do, even if it might have been done for the wrong reasons. There was no doubt in my mind that segregation was wrong and that every person deserved to be treated equally regardless of the color of his or her skin. Moreover, it goes without saying that I knew recruiting black players would give me a chance to have a better basketball team. I knew that we were one of the last junior college teams in the state to have an all-white team and I knew that adding black athletes would help us be more competitive. So I decided for a variety of reasons to use my best efforts to ensure that in the 1970–71 basketball season, the Mustang team would have black players.

The other recruiting charge I received that year was from my mother, and it had nothing to do with basketball. She had asked me to come by their home in Birmingham for a home-cooked meal, which I of course did, and after dinner we were talking in the living room, watching with amusement as my dad fell asleep in his favorite easy chair. Then she got to the real reason she had invited me. "Bill, my cousin Lou called the other day and she said that there is a pretty young lady at their church that you ought to meet. Her name is Vivian," she said, adding, "Lou said her parents are active members of the church and well-respected. She gave me her parents' phone number in case you are interested."

I knew from experience that blind dates don't usually turn out well, especially those arranged by relatives. I tried to change the subject and then I offered several excuses, but my mother was persistent, so I reluctantly agreed to call with the hope that the girl wouldn't be home and I would be off the hook. As it turned out, however, Vivian was home, and she answered the phone. She told me that she didn't go out on blind dates and politely thanked me for asking, but suddenly a feeling came over me that she really might be persuaded to go out with me and maybe I really wanted her to. I asked her to think it over and told her I would call back when I came to Birmingham the following week. This time she agreed to go out with me, and the rest, as they say, is history.

We hit it off very well and I was completely taken with her. I took a summer job as recreational director with the Vestavia Hills Country Club and we saw each other almost every night. Over the course of the summer we discovered that we shared the same values and beliefs and she became convinced that I had a few good qualities, and that with some work on her part, I could be husband material. We got engaged that fall and were married on December 19, 1970. That experience illustrates a rule that served me well from my earliest childhood: "Always listen to your mother."

Now that I think about it, she probably could have given me some words of wisdom on recruiting basketball players, but I guess I forgot to ask. The first black player I attempted to recruit was Sam McCammey, the first African-American to play basketball at Scottsboro High School. He was a six-foot-five forward with a nice medium-range jump shot and good leaping ability. I don't think Sam ever really considered coming to Northeast State because of the racial attitudes and violent history of the surrounding community.

I thought it ironic that he signed with Martin Junior College, located in Pulaski, Tennessee. Pulaski was the birthplace of the Ku Klux Klan and also a bastion of white supremacy, but in Sam's mind things were better up there than on Sand Mountain. Apparently he made a good choice, in more ways than one. After starring at Martin for two years, Sam went on to play his last two years at Oral Roberts University. It would have been great to have Sam as our first black player for two reasons. First of all, he was a fine young man as well as an excellent athlete. And secondly he was known and well-liked in the local area, and his presence would have diffused some of the tension surrounding the desegregation issue. Unfortunately that's not how things worked out.

I contacted a number of other black athletes in Alabama but without any luck. As soon as a prospect realized where Northeast State was located, he quickly lost interest. Mentioning Scottsboro or Sand Mountain created an image of a hostile racial environment that I was not able to overcome, so I began to recruit out-of-state. My first two black signees were Steve Easley and Charles Jackson from Crispus Attucks High School in Indianapolis, Indiana. The school was named for a black patriot who became the first casualty of the American Revolution in 1770 when he was shot and killed in the Boston Massacre. It was also the school where college All-American and NBA Hall of Famer Oscar ("the Big O") Robertson played high school basketball.

At first everything went smoothly for our black players at Northeast State, and I was pleasantly surprised at how well they were accepted by the students. The only complaint that I had came from Steve Easley. He told me that a group of students sitting at another table in the cafeteria were "scoping" him. I had no idea what he was talking about. "What do you mean by that?" I asked. "Coach, 'scoping' means that someone is staring at you," he answered. I told him that if this was the biggest problem we had to deal with, we were in pretty good shape.

However, members of the community generally resented the college having black players and regarded the presence of Steve and Charles as "forced integration." I began to get anonymous phone calls at home expressing outrage about my moving to Alabama and bringing in black players from out-of-state. Many of the callers suggested that there were enough white players around Sand Mountain for a championship team if I were any kind of coach. In some cases the callers made their comments more personal and became quite explicit about the consequences of my behavior, especially later at night. One in particular stands out in my mind: "You are a carpetbaggin' sumabich and if you and those niggers don't get off this mountain, you might all find yourselves at the bottom of the Tennessee River," or words to that effect.

Fortunately we did not encounter any overt acts of violence that year, which I attribute to the fact that we had only two black players on a squad of thirteen. Another reason was that Steve and Charles maintained low profiles and confined their activities to attending classes, studying, and playing basketball. As the season went on I became cautiously optimistic that maybe the extremists were "paper tigers": all talk and no action.

Our team came on strong toward the end of the season, winning six out of our last seven games. Our only loss during that stretch was a 66-64 heartbreaker to Calhoun State, which kept us from qualifying for the state junior college tournament. We finished the season with a record of 16-7, the best overall record in our division and were the number one defensive team in the state. Steve and Charles each had good seasons and both committed to stay at Northeast State for their sophomore year.

Dr. Knox never called me in to discuss the basketball program or ask how Steve and Charles were adjusting to college life; however, he sent word to me indirectly that he wanted me to recruit still more black players. Although I agreed in principle, I was concerned that having a concentration of black athletes in a nearly all-white institution would tend to isolate them from the rest of the student body and would probably attract even more attention from the white extremists. It was my opinion at the time that Dr. Knox realized that young black men and women from Alabama did not want to attend college in an area noted for racial intolerance, and understandably so. Bringing in black athletes from other states could have been his way of playing the "numbers game" so the college could continue to receive funding. Since we had very little communication during this time concerning these matters, I cannot say for sure what his thoughts or intentions were. My hopes were that they were honorable.

Despite my reservations, I signed five new black players. The first four were Charles Patton from Knoxville, Tennessee; Freddie and Jasper Whittemore from Paducah, Kentucky; and Jeff Pettiway from Pensacola, Florida. My fifth signee was Lebron Crayton, whose unusual first name would become a household word almost forty years later when the manchild Lebron James was drafted out of high school in 2003 by the Cleveland Cavaliers of the NBA and immediately became a superstar, but there is no connection between the two players.

Our Lebron, who played basketball at City High School in Chattanooga, would actually never set foot on a college basketball court, but he will always have a place in my heart. I was aware that Lebron had developed a knee problem during his senior year at City High and had worn a knee brace for the entire season. He still had an outstanding year, averaging eighteen points and six rebounds per game. His coach told me during the recruiting process that he thought Lebron would probably have to have an operation on his knee at the conclusion of the season.

As I expected, after a post-season trip to an orthopedic surgeon, Lebron was scheduled for knee surgery in late April. I anticipated his having the usual cartilage problems but fully expected him to be back at full speed in a few months and ready to play when the season began. I went to Erlanger Hospital in Chattanooga on April 28 to be with him when he came out of surgery. I was sitting in the waiting room with his mother when the surgeon came to the waiting room to give her the results of the surgery. I could tell that things had not gone well. She just kept saying, "No! No! No!" I could not imagine what had happened. After talking with the surgeon a little longer, Mrs. Crayton went over to the corner of the waiting room and leaned against the wall, sobbing uncontrollably.

I approached the surgeon and told him that I was the basketball coach at Northeast State where Lebron had a basketball scholarship to play in the fall. He gave me a sad look. "Coach, I'm sorry to tell you that Lebron will not be playing any more basketball. We have found cancer in the knee where we thought he only had a torn cartilage, and our only option is to amputate his leg just above his knee," he said. "Freddie

Steinmark, a defensive back at the University of Texas, had the same problem. As you probably know, they had to amputate his leg. It will have to be Lebron's choice, but unless we amputate, he will probably not survive." I was stunned. It was beyond comprehension that a strong young man like Lebron, in the prime of his life, was about to lose his leg. After explaining a few more details related to Lebron's condition, the doctor walked slowly out of the waiting room with his head down.

I went over to express my sympathy to his mother. She was surrounded by some relatives and was still sobbing continuously. After spending some time with her, I told her I would check with her in the next few days to see what decision Lebron was going to make. I just could not make myself use the word "amputation." After that, I excused myself and left the room. I called her the next day and she told me that Lebron had decided to go ahead with the amputation of his leg. I told her how sorry I was and that my thoughts and prayers would be with him. I said that I would come up to Chattanooga on the night before his surgery to visit with him. The last thing that I told her was that we were going to honor Lebron's scholarship despite the fact that he was not going to be able to play and if he wanted to, I would like for him to serve as a student coach for our team.

On the evening before his surgery, I arrived at the hospital and went to Lebron's room where I was greeted by Mrs. Crayton. I was surprised by the upbeat atmosphere in the room. Several of his black friends were there along with his girl friend who, to my surprise, was white. I had been exposed to interracial dating when I lived in Ohio but had not seen much of this in the Deep South. Lebron was joking while his girl friend was at his side holding his hand. I was amazed at how well he was handling this very difficult time in his life. He was talking with his girl friend about how he was going to make up for losing a leg by lifting weights and become as strong as he could in the remaining limbs of his body.

After talking to Mrs. Crayton for a few minutes, I went over to his bed. "Lebron, I just want to let you know that we plan to honor the scholarship offer that we made to you. I would like for you to help me as a student-coach when you come to school this fall," I said. He seemed delighted. "Coach, I appreciate the offer and I will take you up on it," he answered. "I would be honored to help you coach the Mustangs next season."

Our conversation was interrupted by a knock on the door. It was a sportswriter and photographer from one of the Chattanooga newspapers that had covered Lebron's high school team. The writer asked if he could interview Lebron and take a picture for a newspaper article. My first reaction was that the sportswriter was attempting to capitalize on the family's tragedy, but Mrs. Crayton and Lebron were agreeable. Lebron related how what he thought was torn cartilage had turned out to be cancer and although his leg would have to be amputated, I was going to honor his scholarship and that he was planning to attend Northeast State as a student coach. The photographer took a picture of Lebron, his high school coach, and me. The article and picture were put on the wire service and ran in many of the newspapers throughout the United States. I even got a call from my cousin who lived in St. Petersburg, Florida, concerning the article. She had seen it in her local newspaper.

The surgery was successful and Lebron made a relatively quick recovery. When he reported to Northeast State for fall registration in early September, I was surprised to see that he had decided to use crutches rather that an artificial leg. When I asked him the reason for this, he told me that he could not get used to it. Being the good athlete that he was, he was able to get around on the crutches very well despite his handicap. I would like to say that everything went well for Lebron in life from then on, but it simply would not be the truth. He did a good job in his position as student coach at first. The players reacted well to him. They all respected how he was dealing with his situation and were inspired by his courage and determination. Things went well during pre-season practice but once the regular season started, Lebron went into depression. I think that seeing his teammates playing and competing and knowing that he would never be able to participate was too much for him to handle.

I met with him numerous times, but to no avail. He sank deeper into depression and did not return to school for the second semester, and I received reports that he was using drugs. I called him at his home in Chattanooga many times, but he never returned my calls. Almost one year from the day his leg was amputated, one of my players told me that he had read in the *Chattanooga News-Free Press* that Lebron had been arrested on drug charges. I never found out if this information was factual, but given the circumstances of Lebron's emotional and physical pain, it would not have been unreasonable. I also heard that Freddie Steinmark, the Texas defensive back, had died of cancer. I wondered if both would have been better off if their legs had not been amputated. Some time later, I heard about Lebron for the last time: He had died of cancer.

Meanwhile, our basketball team seemed to be headed for another successful year. Our players, both black and white, had developed the kind of closeness that leads to success on the court, and when we went home for Christmas break our record was nine wins and two losses. In January we picked up where we had left off by winning our first four conference games, and appeared to be in position to challenge Walker Junior College, the perennial conference powerhouse, for first place in our division. Despite the fact that we had now had eight black players on our squad, the reaction from the white community was not much different from that of a year before, and I had pretty much become accustomed to the late-night phone calls. The expression "everything seemed to be going so well" is often used to describe a time just before something really bad happens. And before the month was half over, it did.

There was a small restaurant located directly across the highway from the Northeast State campus, appropriately named the College Corner. It had five tables where patrons could come in, sit down, and order their meals, as well as a take-out counter. The restaurant was near a house on the Northeast State campus where six of our players lived. The players who lived in the house ate breakfast and lunch in the school cafeteria during the school week and got their evening meals at the restaurant on Monday through Friday and on weekends. One Tuesday night four of our players drove together to the restaurant. Two of the four, Steve Easley and Charles Jackson, were black.

Even though the Civil Rights Act that desegregated public accommodations had been in effect for six years, the players had no interest in making a statement by sitting at a table. All they wanted was to order their suppers and take them home to eat. While waiting for their orders at the take-out counter, two white men came in and got in line behind Steve and Charles.

They were wearing flannel shirts and dirty blue jeans, and their speech and demeanor identified them as typical Southern "good ole boys," although the less polite term "redneck" turned out to be more accurate.

The larger of the two men was the first to speak. "I didn't know that they served niggers in this restaurant," he said contemptuously. "I hope that they sanitize the plates and eating utensils that they use because I don't want to get any nigger germs the next time I eat here." Both men then laughed uproariously. Neither Steve nor Charles reacted to the provocation. The two white players, Jack Newton and Dean Breeden, attempted to defuse the situation. "Look guys, we're basketball players at Northeast State and all we want is to get some take-out food. We don't want any trouble," Jack explained. The man that had made the racial slur glared hatefully at Jack and Dean. "You two are nigger lovers and I'm not interested in anything that y'all have to say. Besides, y'all are nothing more than white niggers yourself," he said. By that time Charles and Steve had paid for their take-out orders and began walking out the door. One of the men then shouted, "Hey, nigger boys, where do you think you're going?" Steve and Charles kept walking toward their car in the parking lot. The white men left the restaurant and sprinted out to the parking lot and blocked Steve and Charles from getting into their car.

The man who had been doing the talking was, by then, completely enraged. "We ain't through talking to you two nigger boys yet," he yelled at the top of his voice. "When a white person is talking, nigger boys are supposed to stop and listen. I want to make one thing perfectly clear. We have a rule on Sand Mountain that says there are no niggers permitted to live up here and no niggers permitted to be on this mountain for any reason after dark." Charles then said, "Look, man, we are just trying to go to college to get an education and play a little basketball. We don't mean any harm to anyone." His conciliatory remarks inflamed the man even more. "If you don't get your black ass off this mountain immediately, I am going to whip you like a red-headed step-child," he yelled. Charles tried again to calm him down. "All that we are trying to do is get an education and better ourselves," he said quietly. By that time the man was completely out of control.

Without saying another word, he lunged toward Charles and took a vicious swing at him with his right fist. Fortunately, Charles saw it coming and ducked. The man swung so hard that when he failed to connect with his punch, the momentum of the swing caused him to fall flat on his face. Then he got up and made a rush toward Charles, who decked him with a straight right hand to the jaw. After that, the second man charged Charles. Steve came to his defense and the brawl was on. Steve and Charles were both bigger, younger and in better shape than their attackers. Steve was six feet, three inches and weighed 205 pounds and Charles was a little smaller at six feet, two inches and 195 pounds. In less than a minute, both white men were on the ground moaning in pain. Steve, Charles, Jack, and Dean all got in the car immediately after the fight and drove quickly back to the campus. They knew that the men who had attacked them probably had guns in their car and that the way they saw things, the best way to deal with "uppity niggers" and their white friends was a bullet to the head.

Once they got to the house, Jack called me at my home in Scottsboro and told me what had happened. He was concerned that the men would enlist their friends and come after Charles and Steve. I agreed. Since they didn't have cars, Jack helped them pack up their stuff and drove them to a small home in Scottsboro where I had housed some other players. I spent a sleepless night, knowing that this incident was going to set off a major backlash in the white community.

When I arrived at school the next morning, I had a phone message from Dr. Kent Horner, the dean of students, asking me to meet him at his office as soon as I got on campus. When I got there, Kent, who was normally affable and in good spirits, was clearly shaken. "Bill, we had some major trouble on campus last night. A mob from the community came to campus looking for two of your black players," he said. "Our campus police handled the situation, but you know most of them [the policemen] probably did not want blacks to be here in the first place," he continued. He pointed out to me that they were actually employed by a nearby community which had contracted with Northeast State to provide campus security. "The fact is, they probably wanted to join in with the mob," he said sadly. As it turned out, neither the mob nor the police officers knew exactly where the players lived, a fact which probably averted a violent confrontation, but I knew that this was not the last of it.

I already knew how most of the officers felt about me. Many of the people in the community believed that I was the "outsider" who was responsible for bringing the blacks in to attend the college and play basketball and that I should therefore be the one who shouldered the blame for any problems. It was logical to assume that the officers from the local area would feel the same way. One night shortly after my first black players arrived on campus, Vivian and I stopped by the gym to pick up a grade book I had forgotten to take home with me. When we were leaving the gym parking lot, two officers blocked the exit with their patrol car and accused me of breaking in the gym. Even after I showed them my ID, they continued to detain us until I insisted that they take us to the administration building, where the night custodian identified me. Then they took off in their patrol car and left Vivian and me to walk back to our car. I was sure they knew who I was and that they had refused to accept my ID just to harass me; on the other hand, maybe I should have given them the benefit of the doubt because I was later told that neither of them could read. The thought that my security and the security of my players was in the hands of policemen who were possibly both racist and illiterate still gives me a chill.

I told Dr. Horner about the fight at the College Corner Restaurant and explained how Charles and Steve had tried to avoid the confrontation but were forced to protect themselves. I also told him that I had temporarily moved the two black players out of the campus house. He told me he agreed with my decision. "It probably will be just a matter of time before that mob that was out here last night finds out where Steve and Charles were living," he said. Then he went on to reiterate his opinion that our campus security could not be counted on to protect black players. "For all I know, they might be members of the Ku Klux Klan themselves," he added. I could tell he was deeply discouraged over what had happened and was afraid the situation would get worse. How much worse neither of us could have imagined.

Fire on the Mountain

"And we are here as on a darkling plain,
swept with confused alarms of struggle and flight, where
ignorant armies clash by night."
—Matthew Arnold
In *Dover Beach*

That trouble lay ahead was a virtual certainty. The only questions were when, where, and how bad. But life (I hoped) and the basketball season had to go on. We had a road game at Gadsden State the next night. I thought about the irony of playing a team that was nicknamed the "Confederates." Surprisingly our team had put the events of the previous night behind them and we came away with a two-point win over a very good team. After a post game meal in Gadsden, we had an enjoyable ride back to campus. I was halfway expecting to see an angry mob waiting for us, but when we arrived at the gym, the parking lot was empty except for a few players' cars. After a brief team meeting on the bus to go over the practice time for the next day and conclude several other housekeeping affairs, I congratulated the team on its efforts and said that I would see them the next day. I then got in my car and drove home, pleased with the win and happy that there had been no trouble when we returned.

When I pulled into the driveway at my home, Vivian met me at the door with a concerned look on her face. "Bill, I just got a phone call from Jack Newton. He sounded very upset and wants you to call him immediately," she said. "He wouldn't say what the problem was." I had not told her about the recent incident. We had been married less than a year and I did not want to start our married life with her worrying about my safety.

I assured her I could handle whatever it was and told her not to worry. Then I went into my office in our home and shut the door to call Jack. I could tell by his voice when he answered the phone that something bad had happened. He told me that when he had reached the front porch of the house—the same one we had moved Steve and Charles out of—there was a strong smell of gas. After he had opened the front door, he had started to turn on the light switch in the living room, but Dean had reached over and grabbed his hand. The smell was even stronger and Dean was evidently pretty sure it was natural gas. After they located a flashlight, they had begun to investigate. As the beam swept across the living room wall, it appeared that someone had left a sign on the mantel over the fireplace. When the beam was focused back, it illuminated the words, "Die Niggers" on the sign.

When they went into the kitchen to check on the source of the gas, they discovered that someone had turned on the oven and all four eyes of the gas stove. I told Jack that both he and Dean should get out of the house immediately. For all I knew the intruders might have also placed bombs. I instructed them and the other two white players who were still living on campus to meet me in the parking lot of Scottsboro High School. Meanwhile I made arrangements for all four to move in temporarily with some other players who were living in a mobile home on the outskirts of Scottsboro.

I knew from my own experience that Dean might well have saved Jack's life that night by stopping him from turning on the lights. When I was fourteen, I accidentally set off a gas explosion in the kitchen of our home. My mother had taught me a little about cooking and I was about to prepare my first meal of hamburgers and French fries. I turned on one of the eyes and when I was not able to light it, I turned another and then another until I heard the whooshing sound of gas igniting and saw the familiar circle of blue light around the element. As I was watching my hamburger sizzle, I heard our dogs, Denny and Rex, barking in the back yard. I started out to investigate and the last thing I remember is getting about half-way through the screen door. When I came to, I was lying on my back in the yard and Denny and Rex were licking my face. What had happened was that I had not turned off the eyes that didn't ignite, which caused the gas to build up and erupt in an explosion. Dazed, but unhurt, I went back inside to find the stove blown apart and the kitchen in shambles.

What I saw was very likely what would have happened if Jack had flipped the light switch; it's the reason safety regulations say never to turn on an electrical device when the odor of gas is present. My mother was appalled when she saw what had happened to her kitchen, but she was so happy I had not been injured or killed that instead of taking any disciplinary action, she gave me a big hug and said a prayer of thanksgiving. Whether it was divine intervention that caused Denny and Rex to bark so I would leave the kitchen or that caused Dean to take Jack's hand off the light switch is something we cannot know. The Scriptures, however, tell us that the Lord works in mysterious ways.

After going to campus and looking around the house for a few minutes, I decided to talk to Dr. Horner, who by then was one of the few people on campus that I felt that I could count on. It appeared to me that many of the others were unapologetic segregationists. Dr. Knox, the president, was "officially" committed to a policy of equal opportunity, and my activities to integrate the athletic program and student body seemed to have, at a minimum, his tacit approval. As to whether or not I was successful or my players and I got run out of town by an angry mob, it was my impression that I was pretty much left to fend for myself.

After telling Dr. Horner about the attempted murder of the players in the house, he stated, "Bill, this is a bad situation. You did the right thing by getting all of the players out of the house and moving them to Scottsboro immediately. I think that you and your players should keep a low profile the next few days until things cool down." Despite the fact that I had asked our players to keep a low profile since the beginning of these hostilities and that I knew that we would not get much or any help from the local police concerning this matter, I was surprised by his plan of action. "Kent, I do not think that we can continue to keep a low profile related to this situation," I said. "These people meant to kill our players last night by blowing up the house. They're not going to stop because we are keeping a low profile. Don't you think we should call the police and get them to try to locate these criminals and arrest them?" I asked incredulously. I pointed out that as teachers and administrators our role was "*in loco parentis*," which means literally to act as parents. We discussed the issue for a few more minutes and I posed the question a final time: "Kent, are you sure that keeping a low profile is the only thing we can do? After thinking for a moment he looked at me and said quietly, "Bill, I think it's the best thing to do considering what we are up against." I got up and left his office without saying another word. Kent was a good man and one of the few people who stuck by me through this turbulent time, but his rationale reminded me of a saying attributed to Edmund Burke: "Evil triumphs when good men do nothing."

While walking across campus on the way back to my office in the gym, I felt more alone and vulnerable than at any time in my life to that point. I knew that in countries run by totalitarian dictators, people who were of the wrong color or had the wrong ethnic background or had beliefs that were different from the official party line had to be kept in "safe houses" to protect them from being flushed out of hiding by informants, murdered by thugs, or harassed by the police. But this was not Cuba or North Korea. This was happening in the United States of America.

On the way back to my office, I ran into the school's registrar, Wayne Woods. He had been at the gym looking for me to tell me about something that had recently happened at a new children's home under construction just outside of Huntsville. The home, which was near completion, included an administration building, cafeteria, recreation hall, and boys' and girls' dormitories, and was scheduled to open the following week. The director of the facility had invited him to take a tour of the facility. He and the director had met and driven to the entrance, located about a quarter of a mile from the complex, where they had had to unlock a metal gate. After unlocking the gate, they noticed that there was smoke coming up over the trees on the horizon, which they thought was just some farmer in the area burning brush. After driving up a gravel road they made a final turn and came into a big open area. Everything had been burned to the ground. In the middle of the smoldering ruins of what would have been the children's home, somebody had placed a crudely lettered sign that read: "No niggers allowed."

Since the facility had been constructed with federal funds, the home was required to be open to both black and white children. Apparently some of the local Klansmen or their associates decided that it was better for children to be homeless than to live with those of another race. I thought to myself that at least they burned it down before the children moved in. Listening to this story, it was my impression that Wayne was trying to make a point. My impression was correct. He said, "As a friend, I am telling you that those black players are in a dangerous situation out here on Sand Mountain. You might want to consider telling your black players that it would be better for them to go home before someone gets seriously hurt." I told him I appreciated his concern, but that I believed that people should not be discriminated against because of the color of their skin. "Well, I understand what you are saying but still think there is a good chance that something bad is going to happen," he responded with finality.

The following day I went to the Student Center and took a seat at the faculty dining table where about twelve faculty members and administrators had gathered for our customary midmorning snack. On my way to the table, I noticed that many of the students were staring at me and whispering to each other. As soon as I sat down, an uneasy silence came over the group. The people at the table kept their heads down as if they were focused on finishing their snacks, and then one by one they got up and left. Some of them mumbled something about needing to get back to the office to prepare for a class while others left without saying a word. By the time I finished my donut, everyone except Kent Horner had left. He assured me that the behavior of my colleagues was due to the fact that they were worried about the racial tensions and I should not take it personally. Then he found a reason he needed to be somewhere else and excused himself. Within the space of three minutes, I was the only one left at the table. It was as if I had some kind of contagious disease.

In assessing my situation, it appeared that things were so bad that nobody wanted to get involved or even be seen with me. I decided that if I had to go it alone, so be it; there would be no turning back. Even though I was worried about my own safety and the safety of my wife and players, I wasn't about to give my detractors the satisfaction of showing any fear. But I did decide to take some extra measures to equalize things. I had a 12-gauge double-barrel shotgun, a 20-gauge single-action shotgun, and a .22 rifle at home, but I couldn't very well carry these weapons around with me. The first thing that I did after basketball practice that day was to go into Scottsboro and apply for a permit to carry a pistol. Since the campus police, the city police, and the local thugs were all armed, I might as well be, too.

My first order of business, however, was to talk with my players before practice concerning the seriousness of this situation. When I went into the dressing room for our usual pre-practice meeting, I could tell that the players were concerned. Usually, before I walked through the dressing room door, I could hear them boisterously joking with one another, but today they were silent. The moment I entered, all eyes were on me. Despite the fact that I was only a few years older, they expected me to lead them through the tough times. It was a humbling feeling. After looking around the dressing room at each of them, I said, "Guys, you know that I have always been truthful with you. With that in mind, I am not going to stand here and tell you that things are going great. The truth is that we have a very dangerous situation here. You are integrating a school in an all-white community. You were each told that up front when we recruited you." I went on to tell them that I was proud of them for the way they had conducted themselves, and that Steve and Charles had had no choice but to fight back when they were assaulted at the restaurant. While I expected them to try to walk away from confrontations, they had every right to defend themselves when that wasn't an option.

In regard to the verbal abuse, I advised them to ignore it and not to respond in kind. I also stressed that none of them should try to get even with those who they believed were responsible for the attempts on their lives. Instead, they should let the law take its course. Although I am not one to sermonize, I pointed out that in the Scriptures the Lord says, "Vengeance is mine," and that Christ tells us we are to love our enemies. I did acknowledge that the white extremists who were trying to intimidate them were difficult to love. Finally, I reminded them that we had a game coming up with Brewer State and they had to focus on getting better individually and as a team. The players were not as animated as usual after practice, but they were more upbeat than I had expected. They even engaged in a little gallows humor after I dismissed them. I overheard one of them telling the players who live in the campus house to go outside before they lit their cigarettes, even though they knew that I did not tolerate smoking.

I was in my office trying to collect my thoughts when the four white players who still lived in the campus house, came to visit me. I knew what was on their minds. After making some small talk, I suggested that they live temporarily with friends in Scottsboro until I could arrange for off-campus housing. They seemed greatly relieved that I had already decided to take measures to ensure their safety. They all went back to the campus house after our meeting, gathered their belongings and moved in with friends in Scottsboro until I located permanent housing.

The next day we were scheduled to play Brewer State Junior College in Fayette, Alabama. For safety reasons, I instructed our team bus driver, Geather Ashmore, to pick up the squad in the parking lot of Scottsboro High School rather than at the gym on the campus of Northeast State and to take us back to the high school after the game. The people who had been threatening us probably knew our customary travel plans, and I was concerned that a group of them might be waiting when we returned from Fayette or even ambush our black players when they were driving from the Northeast State gym back to Scottsboro. This later proved to be a wise decision.

To my surprise the team showed no ill effects of all the off-court problems we were having and we won by twenty-two points. When we returned to the high school, there was no one in the parking lot and the players went to their homes without incident. As I drove to the campus the next morning, I was feeling good, both about our performance on the court the previous night and over the fact that the trip to Fayette and back had been uneventful. When I arrived at my office, I was surprised to see Geather waiting outside the door. The look on his face told me that something was wrong.

I invited him in and asked him to tell me what was going on. Geather was so shaken he could hardly talk. "Coach, we have a big problem," he began. "Last night after I let the team off at the high school in Scottsboro, I was stopped on Highway 35 by a bunch of guys just on the other side of Section. They had the road blocked with their cars. I thought there had been an accident and I stopped and got out of the bus to see if I could help. When I got out they came up to the bus, and when they saw it was empty, they wanted to know 'where the niggers were.' When I told them I had let all the players out in Scottsboro, they accused me of being a nigger lover and told me what they would do to me if I kept driving the bus." Then he paused before continuing, "Coach, I'm pretty sure they had guns."

Then he swallowed hard and said, "I think you know me well enough to know that I am not afraid of anybody, but I'm worried about what might happen to my family." I could tell that he was about at the breaking point. Then he looked down at the floor. "Coach, I'm going to have to think long and hard about staying on as your bus driver," he said sadly. He told me about a recent incident in which one of the men in the group had gotten angry at someone and had taken a bulldozer to his house late one night, driving it through his living room. "The guy he was mad at was white," he said incredulously. "There's no telling what he might do to a black person." After listening to his story I told him that I appreciated him for being thoughtful of and friendly to all our players, regardless of whether they were black or white. I went on to assure him that if he felt he could not drive the bus for us any longer, we would understand.

My three-day waiting period for a gun permit had ended,

and at lunch that day, I went to Scottsboro to purchase a pistol and some ammunition. Since I was not going to get any protection from the police or the school, I felt I had no choice but to take things into my own hands. If a mob with murderous intentions stopped our bus, I was going to take a few of them out before they got us. I didn't think this was the Christian thing to do, but neither did it seem right that I should sit by and watch as our black players were snatched from the bus and taken away to be beaten or even murdered. I was responsible for the safety of my players —they were the innocents in this situation—and this seemed to be the only option I had. My dad had told me when I was a boy never to point a gun at someone unless I planned to kill him. I made the decision that if someone attacked one of my players or my wife, I would shoot to kill. The only question I had in my mind was whether to warn the person or shoot first and ask questions later. When I got home from work that day, I went into the woods behind my house, loaded my pistol, and took target practice.

My major focus, however, continued to be on avoiding potentially dangerous situations. Although off-campus housing provided a measure of safety for individual players, it was obvious that each home game was an open invitation to the local white extremists to show up, and a violent confrontation involving the whole team was a virtual certainty. I knew that the local rednecks typically got together after work to organize for carrying out whatever terrorist activities had been planned for the night. While I couldn't stop them from plotting against us, I decided to at least disrupt their schedule by changing the starting times for our games from 7:30 P.M. to 1:00 P.M., beginning with Snead State the following day.

Although the players were under a great deal of stress over a situation that seemed to be going from bad to worse, they continued to perform well on the court. We beat Snead State 80-62, putting us in a tie for first place in our division. The game ended about 3:00 and the players were safe in their homes an hour later. I thought to myself that it had been a good day: We had a good win and there had been no racial trouble. But the day was not over. That night I got a call from Kent Horner. He got straight to the point: "Bill, a mob showed up at the gym about 7:30 this evening looking for the black players and were really enraged when they found out the game had already been played. You and I both know they'll be back."

I decided it was time to visit with Dr. Knox and give him a report on the overall state of the basketball program, including the racial problems, but also covering a number of positive items. During our meeting he didn't once compliment my players for staying the course; he didn't say anything about our winning record, nor did he express appreciation to me for my good efforts in staying one step ahead of the mob. He did agree to arrange for security at our remaining home games, although he pointed out that the local police were probably displeased that I had black players on the team and might not go out of their way to protect them. When I left the meeting, it was my impression that he was more annoyed than anything else. Maybe if I hadn't let my players off in Scottsboro several nights earlier, the mob could have killed them or at least intimidated them into leaving. Now they were showing up on the campus and creating a major inconvenience. It was all my fault.

I was continually reminded that things had been fine until I started recruiting black basketball players. The mass exodus from the faculty table when I sat down for coffee and donuts had become a daily ritual. Even the people who were sympathetic to my situation became nervous when others saw us together. In the community, perfect strangers would give me dirty looks, sometimes adding a disparaging comment to make sure that I knew I was held in low esteem. One day, on my way home, I turned into a gas station and the driver of a beat-up car that had been following me also turned, pulling his car in front of mine to block me in. When he got out of his car, I could see that he was displeased, and I thought maybe he was going to complain about the way I had been driving or that I had failed to give a proper turn signal, so I rolled down my car window to hear him out. But that wasn't what was on his mind. "We don't allow niggers to live on Sand Mountain and we damn sure don't want niggers playing basketball at our college," he screamed in a demented rage, drenching me with saliva and tobacco juice.

I took out my handkerchief and wiped my face. My first thought was to get out of the car and punch him in the mouth, but I decided instead to act as if we were having a normal conversation. "Thank you for your comments," I said politely. "I will take everything you said into consideration." This was not what he had expected and he stood there with his mouth open. When I started the engine he regained his composure for a parting shot. "I know what your car looks like," he yelled as I drove away. I thought to myself that it was only a matter of time until he would find my car unattended and slash the tires. As I would later discover, slashing my tires was probably not what he had in mind.

During that time I felt a great sense of isolation from the community and even from the church that Vivian and I attended. In other places I had lived, I could visit with my pastor and ask for guidance and advice during troubled times, and I could always count on members of the congregation for a friendly hug or kind word. But I was offered little comfort and no support whatever. As was the case in Birmingham when I was a child, many of the church members believed blacks to be an inferior race and that segregation was ordained by God. While it was our duty to send missionaries to Africa to convert black people to Christianity, we were not supposed to have anything to do with them socially, and the prospect of allowing them to worship in a white church was unthinkable.

I felt that the pastor, along with some of the church members, regarded me as a misguided social liberal from Ohio who was causing problems for the community. They had to tolerate me because I was white, but other than that, few wanted to have anything to do with me. There were exceptions, of course. We became good friends with Sam Holland, a local boy establishing a new dental practice, and his wife, Mary Ann, who taught at Scottsboro High School with Vivian. We also became close to Leroy Gist, the local photographer, whose family owned a great little frame shop in Scottsboro. We were regular customers and Vivian taught one of their daughters.

My only physical diversion was tennis. I had not played as a kid, but had taken courses as part of my college curriculum, so I had developed considerable skills, and even played on the varsity while I was a student at Cedarville and Howard. The problem was, there were very few people in the area that played tennis and none who could play at my level. Moreover, it was questionable that anyone, regardless of his or her skills, would want to associate with me. But, as luck would have it, a faculty member at Northeast State suggested that I contact a man from Fort Payne who was considered one of the best tennis players in the area. So I called him, and after a few games, we decided that not only did we match up well on the tennis court, but we also enjoyed each other's company.

We had been playing for several weeks at the public courts in Rainsville when one of my friends on the faculty stopped by my office. After a minute or so of small talk, he got around to what was obviously on his mind. "Bill, I think you should know that the guy that you are playing tennis with is one of the leaders of the Ku Klux Klan for northeast Alabama," he said. My friend didn't indicate what he was called but someone told me later he was the Grand Dragon. I wondered to myself if my tennis partner knew about my situation. As if he were reading my thoughts, my friend continued. "I feel sure that he holds you responsible for bringing black players to Northeast State." That was a reality check for me.

In spite of my friend's revelation, I decided to keep playing tennis with the alleged Klan leader. I would like to say that we had deep philosophical discussions about racial issues, but the truth is, neither of us ever brought up the subject. We put our differences aside and enjoyed friendly competition. I often wondered how the good ole boys back at the Klavern felt about their leader playing tennis with the enemy. After all, it was people like me that they were supposed to run out of town to protect the Southern way of life. But I never learned the answer to that question. As for my tennis partner and me, we observed an unspoken truce for a few hours every week and then went our separate ways. He had his job; I had mine.

It did feel strange knowing that if my tennis partner was indeed the leader of the Ku Klux Klan, that he most likely received regular reports on what was going on at Northeast State. I'm quite certain he knew about the attempt to blow up the house, the incidents on campus and the ambush of the bus. Possibly he was in on the planning and even gave the orders, but that is only speculation. I knew the Klan maintained a presence at colleges and schools where integration efforts were in progress for the purpose of instilling fear, even using violent means, if warranted, to intimidate both blacks who were exercising their rights and the whites who collaborated with them. It was during this time that Coach Bear Bryant began recruiting black football players under the watchful eye of Robert Shelton, the Imperial Wizard of the Ku Klux Klan. Apparently Bryant rated an Imperial Wizard because he ran a Division I program while I had to settle for a Grand Dragon. Or so I was told, anyway; I never knew for sure what his title was. Well, at least he was a good tennis player.

One of the major justifications of segregation by the Klan and its sympathizers was the idea that young black men had insatiable sexual desires. Unless they were restrained by intimidation and the threat of being lynched, they would indulge these desires with white women. The classic but blatantly racist 1915 film, *The Birth of a Nation*, reinforced this sterotype. The film's character Flora, a young virgin, throws herself off a cliff to avoid being raped by the black character Gus, described as "a renegade, a product of the vicious doctrines spread by the carpetbaggers."

An incident involving my black players and local white girls was the only foolish situation we got ourselves into that season. We avoided trouble, but not by much. As if I needed something else to worry about, I learned that three of my players were going out most nights to see white girls who lived in a mobile home park on Sand Mountain. I met with the team and told them that while I had no personal bias against interracial dating, they were endangering not only their own lives, but also the lives of the girls. I pointed out that the word would get around and as soon as it did, all hell would break loose. I suggested that they decide if their social lives were worth the risk of becoming latter-day Scottsboro Boys and act accordingly. It bothered me that I had to caution them against doing something that was well within their rights, but in this case I believed that discretion was the better part of valor. I never again brought up the subject and to my knowledge, they followed my advice.

Then it was back to coaching basketball. I tried to keep my mind off the distractions so I could devote my mental energies to what I had been hired to do. I went about my regular routines of practice, running our game plans, counseling players, and trying to keep the team focused on succeeding, both in their studies and on the court. The threatening phone calls came on a frequent basis and I continued to encounter hostility from perfect strangers along with some who we thought were our friends. Several times when I was driving home from work, somebody would try to run me off the road. Local terrorists continued to stalk the players and set up ambushes. But in spite of their best-laid plans, they always ended up at the wrong place or came at the wrong time.

Although we were in what amounted to a war zone and the players were under constant mental stress, they never succumbed to the pressure. Rather, the adversity seemed to inspire them and as the season wound down, they were playing at the top of their games. They had also formed a close bond among themselves. One of my best memories of that time was when the players gathered to watch *Brian's Song*, a made-for-TV movie about the friendship between Chicago Bears football players

Brian Piccolo who was white and Gayle Sayers who was black. In my mind's eye I can still see Steve Easley, our team tough guy, as his eyes filled up with tears during the ending when Piccolo died of cancer. We finished the regular season with a record of 20-6 and were co-champions of our division.

In the quarter-finals of the Alabama Junior College State Tournament, we beat Patrick Henry Junior College by a score of 74-70. Our opponent in the semi-finals was the defending state champions, Jefferson State Junior College. We were behind by one point with fifteen seconds left but had possession of the ball. Dean Breeden, one of our best players, missed a wide-open shot close to the basket and Jefferson State rebounded. As they passed the ball around to run out the clock, our season began to run through my mind—the fight at the College Corner, the attempt to blow up the players' house, the angry mobs, and the other abuse directed at my players and me, all over the fact that fifteen years after the Supreme Court had ruled segregation in public schools was unconstitutional and six years after the passage of the Civil Rights Act, we had black players on our basketball team.

I was lost in my thoughts for what seemed like hours, but in reality it could not have been more than a few seconds. Then the loud, discordant buzzer sounded, bringing me back to reality and signifying the end of the game, and for us, the tournament. As I watched the players on both teams shake hands and offer congratulations to each other on a hard-fought game, I wondered what to make of everything we had experienced. The answer would be a long time coming. For then, all I knew for sure was that for good or bad, this season was in the books.

With that season finally behind me, I spent a few days

reflecting on what had been accomplished. In regard to basketball, I felt we had done very well. We finished the regular season with twenty wins and only six losses. Dean Breeden and Charlie Patton were selected to the All-Alabama Junior College Team, and Freddie Whittemore received an honorable mention. Jeff Pettiway was named to the Alabama Junior College State Tournament All-Tournament Team. Jack Newton, Steve Easley, Charles Jackson, and Dean Breeden signed scholarships with four-year colleges. I was named Northern Division Coach of the Year. My overall coaching record of 105-48 was the best in the six-year history of the Alabama Junior College Conference.

As to whether we were able to change attitudes and convince people that African-Americans should be treated with dignity and respect and have equal opportunities in education and sports, I would have to say that the reviews were mixed. The students accepted the black players, cheered for them on the court, and generally made them feel welcome to participate in the college experience. Unfortunately, this was not always the case with the faculty, administration, or the community.

After the season ended, things calmed down considerably, although I did continue to receive threatening phone calls at home. We decided to keep housing our players in Scottsboro rather than moving them back to the campus. Our black players lived in the small neighborhood that was located next to the railroad tracks, generally with or next door to black families. I suspended spring work-outs so that our players would be on Sand Mountain only during class time. It might be assumed by some that I had finally accepted the rule that blacks were allowed on Sand Mountain only during daylight hours, but the truth was that I was afraid they might be ambushed on the road if they had to travel back to Scottsboro at night.

Neither Dr. Knox nor his inner circle of administrators offered to meet with me to develop a strategy to deal with the problem of racial unrest; in fact, they didn't even acknowledge that there was a problem. No administrator other than Kent Horner had much to do with me other than to say hello or engage in brief small talk. After several weeks of being ignored, I decided to take things into my own hands and do what I thought best for my returning players. I met with them individually and informed them that I could not in good conscience guarantee their safety if they returned to Northeast State to play for the 1972–73 season. I expressed my personal appreciation to them for their performance on the court, for their loyalty to the team, for the way they had conducted themselves, and for staying the course. I also told them that if they decided to leave Northeast State, I would do my best to arrange a transfer to another college. They were asked to think it over for a few days and come by and let me know individually what they had decided to do.

Three black freshmen players made the decision to leave. Charlie Patton, our leading scorer, transferred to Cleveland State Junior College, and Jeff Pettiway, one of the top junior college point guards in the state, signed to play at Lee College. Back-up center Ron West, a walk-on, said he planned to leave whether or not he was able to play at another college. Only Freddie and Jasper Whittemore elected to return for the following season.

To say that 1972–73 was a rebuilding year would be an understatement. We had lost eight players, all of whom had been starters at one time or another. Freddie Whittemore, who had averaged eleven points and twelve rebounds per game, was our only experienced player, and only two others had any game experience at all. We added fourteen freshmen to the squad to fill out the roster. The only black player among these new recruits was Clint Turner from Mayfield, Kentucky. Even though I told Clint up-front about all of the problems that we had had the previous year, he still wanted to play for Northeast State.

Despite living in a racially charged atmosphere, neither the players nor I experienced any overt acts of violence during the early fall, and we began the season without incident. I had even begun to feel that we had turned a corner, at least in regard to acts of violence by the extremist elements in the community. This interlude of relative calm ended on December 4, 1972.

When I got home, Vivian met me at the door and asked me if I had heard the news. She told me that Loy Campbell, a local attorney and former neighbor, had been critically injured that morning when a bomb went off in his car on a street near the elementary school where his daughter was a student. When the ambulance arrived, the emergency medical technicians discovered that both of his legs had been blown off and he was going into shock. By some miracle they were able to save his life and get him to the hospital. It was later discovered that he usually gave his daughter a ride to school, but he had overslept that day, and she had walked. Obviously the person who put the bomb in the car meant to kill both of them.

Because my wife and I were living in the city at the time of this bombing, and my wife remembers hearing the blast and feeling the shock from it in her high school classroom that morning, I have taken an interest in reading various accounts written about it. The best I've found is Byron Woodfin's book, *Lay Down with Dogs*, and most of my information about Bynum should be attributed to Woodfin.

Most people suspected that Hugh Otis Bynum was involved. Bynum, an eccentric local millionaire, had a twenty-year history of going after anyone who displeased him and had been personally involved in a string of violent acts including shootings, stabbings, and assaults and was thought to have arranged others. Only a few of these incidents had led to charges, which were usually dropped, although once he did receive probation for stabbing a man. As was the case in many towns in the South, the local authorities tended to tread lightly around white men with money and connections. Bynum, of course, had another advantage. Very few witnesses to his violent acts were willing to risk their lives by coming forward.

Bynum especially hated black people. Once he saw a black boy holding a puppy and told him to put the puppy down and move aside. Then he shot the puppy's head off with a shotgun. When the boy's father threatened to file charges against him, Bynum went to the man's job site with a gun, where his coworkers saved his life by hiding him until Bynum left. Charges were never filed. Shortly before the bombing, Bynum had shot and seriously wounded two black teenagers who were walking across some property he owned. Although Bynum was arrested, the black community understandably doubted that he would ever be tried and convicted, and organized protests. During this time, several barns and a house owned by Bynum and members of his family were torched, apparently in retaliation for the shooting of the black teenagers. Two men were arrested and charged with arson.

Loy Campbell was appointed by the court to defend the suspected arsonists. Although he had been Bynum's former attorney and had even prepared his will, his defending "the enemy" infuriated Bynum. He and Campbell became estranged, although Campbell really had no choice; he was required to take the case. Rather than merely representing the men and possibly working out a plea bargain, however, Campbell further enraged Bynum by mounting a vigorous defense and earning the men an acquittal. The obvious logical assumption is that Bynum then arranged to have the bomb placed in Campbell's car in retaliation.

Knowing of Bynum's violent nature and hatred of blacks, it did cross my mind to wonder if I was on his list. That night I got a phone call. "You know what happened to Loy Campbell," said the caller in a low voice. "You might be next, and if you don't get those niggers off your basketball team and off Sand Mountain, you can bank on it," he continued. Then he hung up and I stood there in stunned silence listening to the dial tone. I'm fairly sure I recognized the voice. Getting my tires slashed now seemed the least of my worries.

My concern about being on Bynum's hit list was more than speculation. It was eventually revealed that Bynum had hired his friend Billy Ray McCrary, a career criminal, to find a hit man to kill not only Loy Campbell, but also Jackson County Sheriff Bob Collins, former District Attorney Jay Black, Scottsboro Mayor John Reid, and car dealer Sam Holland. These men had all incurred his displeasure over the years for a series of real and imagined offenses that ranged from upholding the law to suggesting that the community improve its image of racial intolerance. There were three other unnamed people on Bynum's hit list. It became clear that the bombing of Loy Campbell's car was not an isolated incident; rather it was part of an elaborate plot to assassinate a group of people that I had ample reason to believe included me.

Naturally I took every precaution that came to mind. I put strips of tape around the edges of the garage door and checked every morning to be sure that nobody had gotten in during the night. When I had to leave my car in a parking lot or on the street, I always opened the hood to check for explosive devices and instructed Vivian to do the same thing. (I'm not sure she did what I told her, but I did instruct her to nonetheless.)

I made sure we never sat or stood in front of the large picture window in our living room at night so that we wouldn't be in the line of fire if someone shot into the house. I kept a loaded pistol next to my bed. Vivian and I were essentially prisoners in our own home and targets of opportunity the rest of the time.

I would later learn from reading Woodfin's book that my fears were not exaggerated. I discovered that Billy Ray Mc-Crary did indeed hire a hit man to do Bynum's dirty work. His name was Charles Hale and he lived with his girl friend, Darlene Sullivan, in the small community of Pisgah, located on Sand Mountain close to Northeast State. Hale was a known associate of a loosely organized band of thugs who engaged in various illegal activities in the area. It is logical to wonder if some of his associates were not among the individuals who were harassing our black players.

Bynum provided Hale a .30-06 rifle with a scope to do a hit on Sheriff Bob Collins. Bynum asked Hale to take the rifle and hide in the woods adjacent to the sheriff's farm on Tupelo Pike. He prepared him with the information that Collins came out to one of the fields each night to feed his cattle and instructed him to set up in the woods and ambush Collins. Fortunately for Collins, he did not show up to feed his cattle that particular evening and was thus spared.

At Bynum's bidding, Hale planned also to shoot Judge Jay Black through a window at his home in Fort Payne. Hale went so far as to go on a "scouting" trip with Sullivan one night to determine which window would be best to aim at to get Judge Black. Bynum was incensed with Black, who was the prosecutor in his case related to shooting of two black teenagers and he wanted the judge done away with. Despite all of the planning, however, for some unknown reason, Hale did not follow through with his plans. With all of this in mind, I think my concerns related to someone's taking a shot at me through my den window were not unfounded.

Taking into consideration the fact that Hale did plant dynamite in Campbell's car and attempted to put dynamite under the hood of Sheriff Collins's vehicle, added to the fact that I had gotten several threats that I was going to end up like Campbell, I do not consider that my daily routine of checking my and Vivian's cars for bombs to be an overreaction.

My worst fears were confirmed when shortly after I left Northeast State to go to graduate school at the University of Alabama, local Judge John Tally pulled into a gas station in Scottsboro. In those days, gas station attendants not only pumped gas but also checked your oil and water. While checking under the hood, the gas station attendant found what he thought was a soft drink bottle. Upon further examination, however, he discovered wires attached to the bottle's cap. He traced the wires to the vehicle's head lights.

Talley said that his son had noticed the device earlier and thought it was just part of the windshield washer unit. It was later determined that the explosive device, complete with a blasting cap, was wired to explode when the headlights were switched to high beam.

When I came to Northeast State in 1965, the conflict in Vietnam had begun to escalate and would soon drive President Lyndon Johnson from office. By late 1972, President Richard Nixon had been reelected to a second term in a landslide, mainly because he was able to negotiate an end to a war that had cost over fifty thousand American lives. I remember listening to the statement from U.S. Secretary of State Henry Kissinger: "Peace is at hand." On Sand Mountain, however, peace seemed far away.

Wrapping Up and Moving On

I tried to put all of this out of my mind when I was working with the basketball team, but I'm sure that my effectiveness as a coach was diminished. As expected, the team struggled during the early part of the season, but played good defense, which kept us in the games. The offense was inconsistent most of the year but improved dramatically toward the end of the season. We won five of our last six games and finished with a 14-11 record, one win short of qualifying us for the state tournament. It was our seventh-straight winning season. We gave up just 59.9 points a game and finished as the fourth-best defensive team in the nation among junior colleges. Freddie Whittemore, who became the first black captain at Northeast State, averaged 11.8 points and 15.5 rebounds per game, setting the single-season record for the Mustangs.

Even though we still had three black players and one black manager on our squad, the white extremists must have felt that they had won a battle and eventually were going to win the war. To some extent, I had to agree. They were responsible for the provocations and threats that caused several black players to leave the team and led to my decision to move all our players off-campus. They bragged about enforcing the "law" that "no niggers were allowed on Sand Mountain after sundown." In addition to taking the measures I mentioned to protect Vivian and myself, I carried a pistol with me to school every day and on all road games in case a mob tried to ambush the bus. We all had to live under the constant threat of being beaten, shot, kidnapped, or blown up.

By this time, Alabama Attorney General Bill Baxley had taken over the investigation of the bombing of Loy Campbell's car and would eventually head the prosecution team that tried Hugh Otis Bynum for attempted murder. Many people, however, regarded Bynum as a colorful, if eccentric, character and somewhat of a folk hero for his acts of violence against black people, including the shooting of the two black teenagers. They considered Baxley a liberal opportunist who wanted to score political points with black voters. Whether he could ever get a jury to convict Scottsboro's wealthiest citizen was very much in doubt.

On campus, I had virtually no communication with Dr. Knox and most of his administrative staff, and other than a box with my name inscribed in it and a reporting line to them on the official organization chart, I didn't really exist. Members of the faculty and staff treated me politely, speaking when we met in passing, but with a few exceptions, that was about as far as it went. Sometimes a few people would remain at the faculty table when I sat down, but if the number dropped below three or four, they would quickly discover a reason to be somewhere else. Most of the people in the church that we attended seemed to believe that white supremacy was justified on religious grounds. Although generally opposed to violence against blacks, they tended to blame "outside agitators" for creating the problem. Since this term applied to anyone from another state who believed that all people were created equal and that public institutions were supposed to obey the laws of our country, I fit very neatly in this category. Vivian and I had few close friends and our social life was practically nonexistent. The sense of isolation was sometimes overwhelming.

Despite my continual prayers for racial reconciliation to take place through the Christian community, it never happened. Although there were people of faith, including some in my own church, who wanted an end to discrimination, there were not enough of them to form an advocacy group to challenge the status quo. The few churches that took a position on the racial issue tended to be Pentecostal or charismatic, or they were regarded as "liberal"—such as Episcopalians and Roman Catholics. The dominant local denominations—Baptists, Methodists, Presbyterians and Churches of Christ—either advocated segregation or regarded it as a social issue with no religious implications.

After the completion of the 1972–73 basketball season, I contemplated going back to school to begin work toward my doctorate. This would prepare me for my ultimate goal of going into administration, preferably athletic administration, after I retired as a coach. I was not really ready to give up coaching, but the situation was becoming more and more emotionally exhausting, and I did not think I could continue working at Northeast State. It was time for a change.

That spring, I applied for several college basketball coaching jobs that were open but did not get serious consideration for any of them. This puzzled me because I had the best overall coaching record in the Alabama Junior College Conference. My teams had won one state championship, had been the state runners-up on another occasion, had made the final-four in the state tournament another year, and had had seven straight winning seasons.

I soon learned from the coaches' grapevine that college presidents in the state were more turned off by my involvement in the confrontations over bringing in black players than they were impressed by my win-loss record. In their defense, however, their reasons for selecting other candidates probably had little to do with racism because many of the colleges had black players. A coach who would bring in only one or two black players at a time, not attracting any attention from the local extremists and generally keeping the lid on things was more valuable to them than a coach who won a lot of games. Based on my history, it must have been obvious that I was not their guy.

In May of that year, I was admitted to the doctoral program at the University of Alabama and received an assistantship to teach undergraduate physical education classes. Vivian was offered a job teaching high school English at nearby Holt High School. I had planned to inform Dr. Knox as soon as we made a final decision, but he had heard that I might be making plans to leave and sent for me. When I got to his office, he acted as if my resignation were a foregone conclusion; his main interest seemed to be discussing my responsibilities for the rest of the academic year. He didn't thank me for establishing the physical education and intercollegiate basketball programs or express appreciation for my seven years of service or compliment me for having a winning record under adverse circumstances. Maybe his mind was on something else.

Finally, I visited with my players who were returning along with those I had signed for the 1973–74 season. I told them I was leaving and that if they wanted to transfer, I would help them find another place to play. In later years I did not encourage players to transfer when I was planning to leave a school, but I considered this to be a unique situation. It was an emotional experience and I had difficulty holding back the tears.

On August 12, 1973, Vivian and I loaded up our cars and set out for Tuscaloosa. As we drove by the campus one last time, it settled in on me how much I was going to miss coaching. Years later, I would read in Rick Warren's book, *The Purpose-Driven Life*, where he asks the question, "What on earth am I here for?" I am convinced now that one reason God placed me on earth was to coach at Northeast State Junior College and provide an opportunity for black athletes to get a college education and play basketball. In his book, *The Life That You've Always Wanted*, John Ortberg describes the role that adversity plays in one's spiritual growth. When he surveyed hundreds of people concerning the factors that were most significant in their spiritual growth, the number one response was suffering and pain.

He talks about the role of suffering as one of the most neglected issues in spiritual growth, because we do not arrange for it to happen as we might Bible study or prayer. Instead, life inevitably arranges it for us. He suggests that if we are going to mature spiritually, we must look at how suffering benefits us, or at least how to respond to it. I think God used my turbulent times at Northeast State to test my faith and help me become a stronger Christian. James wrote in Hebrews that

"You know that the testing of faith produces endurance; and let endurance have it full effect, so that you can be mature and complete, lacking in nothing." I gained an understanding of His ability to guide and protect me, even when I was unaware of His involvement. In looking back, I sense again how blessed I have been.

But these insights were years away, along with the knowledge that God had planned for me to coach for twenty-two more years—more than three times as many years as I had spent at Northeast State. At that time I wondered what, if anything, I had accomplished. Maybe my players and I had been catalysts for change, and people in the college and community would begin to realize that members of all races should have the opportunity to pursue the American Dream. Or maybe the whole effort would be written off as a failed social experiment and most people would remain committed to the belief that segregation was God's will. Either way, my part there was over. These words from *The Rubaiyat of Omar Khayyam* put it quite well: "The moving finger writes, and having writ, moves on; nor all your piety or wit shall lure it back to cancel half a line, nor your tears wash out a word of it."

Epilogue

"Change is the law of life. And those who look only to the past or present are certain to miss the future."
—JOHN F. KENNEDY
Thirty-fifth U.S. President

When I left Northeast State, it was with the view that not much had changed and that the idea that people of all races should have equal opportunities in education, employment, sports, or anything else might be seen as an intrusion on the "Southern way of life" and would be a long time taking hold in Alabama. In Scottsboro and on Sand Mountain, I was convinced that if attitudes ever changed, it might not be in my lifetime. The element of the community that had made a hero out of Hugh Otis Bynum was not even willing to tolerate a few black basketball players on the college team. But as I would soon discover, change is like the hour hand on a clock. You notice after it has advanced, but you can't see it move.

On Monday, March 3, 1975, it took an all-white jury only five hours to find Hugh Otis Bynum guilty of attempted murder. The judge sentenced Bynum to the state penitentiary where he remained until he died in 1980, never revealing the other names on his hit list. In an ironic twist of fate, he later shared a cell with Robert E. "Dynamite Bob" Chambliss, who was eventually convicted in 1977 for the 1963 Birmingham church bombing in which four black girls died.

Martin Luther King, Jr., had been assassinated while I was at Northeast State, but he was still vilified there and throughout Alabama when I left in 1973. Acknowledging his contributions to society was political suicide, as Albert Brewer learned when he lost a bitter 1970 governor's race to George Wallace. But three years later the Alabama Legislature passed a resolution declaring the section of I-85 leading into Montgomery the "Martin Luther King, Jr., Expressway," even though the U.S. Department of Transportation had a rule against naming parts of the Interstate system for individuals. The state of Alabama, which had been notorious for defying the federal government over enforcement of equal opportunity laws passed as a result of the civil rights movement, was now defying the federal government to honor the leader of the movement. Bizarre.

By the mid-1970s, all public schools and colleges in Alabama had been completely desegregated, and black students participated fully in all aspects of student life from student government to athletics. Outstanding black athletes having to leave the state to play football or basketball at a major college was a fading memory, and the decision faced by blue-chip prospects was whether to sign with Auburn or Alabama. Unfortunately for Auburn, most of them chose Alabama, which dominated both sports until the end of the decade. Even private schools, many of which had been originally established as "segregation academies," began to recruit black athletes.

In 1979, George Wallace made a visit to the Dexter Avenue King Memorial Baptist Church in Montgomery—the church Dr. King pastored during the Montgomery Bus Boycott—to visit with the congregation. He was pushed up the aisle in his wheelchair and spoke: "I have learned what suffering means. I think I can understand something of the pain black people have come to endure. I know I contributed to that pain and I ask for your forgiveness." Wallace, who had risen to national prominence by his opposition to equal opportunity for black citizens, would later win his last race for governor, in 1982, with sixty percent of the black vote.

In 1988, Fred Gainous, an African American, was appointed to head the Alabama Department of Post-Secondary Education, responsible for twenty-nine junior colleges, including Northeast State. Although Dr. Knox had retired, some of the Northeast State staff members who opposed having black students were still there and now reported to a black chancellor.

Today my alma mater, Howard College, once a center for the "convert black people to Christianity but treat them as second-class citizens" school of thought, is home to the Samford University Center for the Study of Law and Education, which sponsors a series of workshops designed to prepare teachers to, in the words of one of their publications, "teach the lessons of justice, hope, authority, perseverance, democracy, citizenship, economic empowerment, and law that are so uniquely woven into the tapestry of the United States of America and the modern civil rights movement."

I realize that it is fashionable to be cynical about how much progress has been made in building the kind of society envisioned by Dr. King, a place "where people are judged by the content of their character rather than the color of their skin." I would never suggest that we have solved all the problems, but those who say that little has been accomplished in the forty years since I arrived at that cornfield on top of Sand Mountain are misguided. While we didn't begin the movement, my players and I were in the trenches and saw action when the issue was still in doubt, and we did start a clock ticking. Maybe we didn't see the hour hand move but it did—and it continues to move today.

Bibliography

Linder, Douglas O. "The Scottsboro Boys' Trials." Famous American Trials. 1999. 2 October, 2006 www.law.umkc.edu/faculty/projects/FTrials.

Ortberg, John. *The Life That You Always Wanted*. Grand Rapids, Michigan: Zondervan Press, 2002.

Warren, Rick. *The Purpose-Driven Life*. Grand Rapids, Michigan: Zondervan Press, 2002.

Woodfin, Byron. *Lay Down with Dogs*. Tuscaloosa, Alabama: University of Alabama Press. 1997.

Index